A Ballerina Prepares

CLASSICAL BALLET VARIATIONS
FOR THE FEMALE DANCER

Margot Fonteyn

poses in a preparation before dancing a classical variation.

———————————————

A Ballerina Prepares

CLASSICAL BALLET VARIATIONS FOR THE FEMALE DANCER

As Taught by

Ludmilla Shollar

and

Anatole Vilzak

Notated by

Laurencia Klaja

DOUBLEDAY & COMPANY, INC., GARDEN CITY, NEW YORK

1982

DRAWINGS BY SELENE FUNG

Design by Beverley Vawter Gallegos

Library of Congress Cataloging in Publication Data
Klaja, Laurencia.   A ballerina prepares.
1. Ballet dancing. I. Fung, Selene. II. Title.
GV1788.K46   792.8'2   AACR2
ISBN: 0-385-15894-7
Library of Congress Catalog Card Number 80–2054

To Madame Ludmilla Shollar
who taught variations to
generations of American dancers

Ludmilla Shollar

𝓕oreword

The day for variations class—Tuesday, I believe—was a very special part of the week. For those of us who were stalwarts, it was a chance to forge our links with the past. We would put on our favorite tunics and, sometimes, arrange flowers in our hair. When Madame Shollar entered, carrying the music for that day's selection, we were prepared to dance, almost literally, in the footsteps of the great ballerinas who came before. In the early forties, Steinway Hall on Fifty-seventh Street was the home of the Vilzak-Shollar studios and, particularly in variations class, a bastion of the way it was done "back when." Variations were never changed to suit the abilities or conceal the defects of the students. Consequently, we attempted the same steps with which women such as Lyubov Egorova, Mathilde Kchessinska, and Olga Preobrajenska had made magic for audiences at the Maryinsky Theatre. When we danced well, and Madame Ariadna Mikéshina would complement us with a particularly spirited accompaniment on the piano, it was certainly performance of a type; and, in this way, we were able to receive the sacrament of that most elusive of performing traditions, the heritage of ballet.

Laurencia Klaja was one of our stalwarts. Some twenty years later, when I was teaching my own variations class at the New York School of Ballet, she would attend, and we would share with new students the fruits of those days with Madame Shollar. At times, when I would have difficulty in remembering a particular passage from a variation, Laurencia would supply me with the missing steps; at times we would compare memories. But, always, the spirit of the original variation and the attempt to reconstruct it literally were there. In this way, she came to the concept that is at the heart of this book.

The handing down of a set of traditions is, in any art, one of the things that continue to lend it the breath of life. To be part of an unbroken aesthetic continuity is an abiding need in many performing artists. But, it is always a tenuous business at best, relying as it so often does on the vagaries of memory. In the ballet, we are doubly challenged by the very "unwritten" nature of the art itself. It is truly a visual and oral tradition. Ballet itself has, naturally, undergone so many changes in the course of its development, that the danger to forget its history, or to be unconsciously led away from it, or, in the case of young people, to be uneducated in it is ever present. What Laurencia Klaja has done in this book is to guard against oblivion and the always-current tendency to lose oneself in the values of the present at the expense of the spirit of the past. Values are at stake here that are as precious as heirlooms. Indeed, that is what these variations are to all of us who love the dance. They were once the property of the great choreographers, the women who first danced them, and the students who came after. Now, thanks to this book, they are, and can always be, yours as well.

New York
August, 1980

BARBARA FALLIS

Contents

Illustrations

Introduction

One of the traditions of ballet is the handing down of training and knowledge directly from teacher to pupil. This book does not seek to break tradition, but to serve as a record of, and guide to, the classical ballet choreography of the past in general and, specifically, as it concerns individual solos created for the female dancer. These solos, which stand on their own as classics, demonstrate various aspects of the technical art of ballet as done *sur les pointes* (on the toes in point shoes), and can serve as a training ground for the young ballerina, once she has had the basic training and developed the strength of her body enough to withstand the rigors of pointe work.

The great teachers and dancers of the past must inevitably vanish with time, and there is always the danger that the original choreography may become lost through the tricks of memory or become changed for one reason or another when it is revived upon the stage. Sometimes this original choreography can only be found in the classroom where it has been left for future generations to preserve as best they can.

The purpose of this book is to attempt to preserve some of these excerpts from the great classical ballets of the last half of the nineteenth and the first part of the twentieth century, and also to serve as a teaching aid to prepare a ballerina for the present-day stage, which relies on the classical ballets as part of its tradition as well as on newer works, thus helping to bridge the chasm that exists between the classroom and the stage.

Most of the book is drawn from the teachings of the Russian ballerina of the Maryinsky Theatre (now the Leningrad Kirov Theatre) and the Diaghilev Ballets Russes, the late Ludmilla Shollar, who was noted for her memory in regard to these dances, or "variations," as they are called in the ballet world. Madame Shollar was the wife of Anatole Vilzak, a noted danseur noble of his time and a favorite partner of many famous ballerinas. Together they founded the Vilzak-Shollar School of Ballet. It was my good fortune to have the opportunity to study with them and thus lay the groundwork for this book. After each class I would go home and try to recall the steps we had studied in the variations given to us that day and would write down whatever I remembered at the moment. The next time we had the same variation, I would check over and add to my notes. In this manner, piece by piece, the correct variation would gradually evolve, somewhat like a jigsaw puzzle.

It has been no easy matter to delve into the past in order to present these variations as accurately as possible. There were questions to be answered as to which ballet a variation originated in, who did the original choreography, who was the composer, and sometimes even which variation it was. Variations may travel from one ballet to another, from female to male dancer, be revised by one choreographer from the choreography of another, or be completely changed with new choreography.

Madame Shollar had collected piano music for all the variations and made sure that we danced the choreography precisely as she was teaching it. Mr. Vilzak also taught variations class at various times during the ensuing years, sometimes teaching the same variations as Madame Shollar did in addition to some from his own dancing experience. The variations were usually demonstrated by their protégée Svetlana Beriosova. When the Vilzaks went to teach at the San Francisco Ballet School, I continued my study of the variations with Barbara Fallis, who had also been their pupil when she was dancing professionally. Attending performances of the great classical ballets was also helpful in tracking down the sources and in noting the changes that had been made over the years.

Madame Shollar encouraged the wearing of a practice tutu of

the powder-puff variety to variations class (which took place once a week), to help us get the feel of and see the line of a costume. These were concoctions in various colors such as pink, blue, white, or black, of organdy or net, which we made ourselves of gathered ruffles, each about an inch longer than the one below it and joined to a panty base. Nowadays, powder-puff tutus have been replaced in variations class by circular chiffon skirts of various lengths. When rehearsing a ballet, a ballerina usually wears a practice skirt that is an approximation of the costume that she will later wear on stage. When called for, props such as a scarf or fan are used. For instance, for the Spanish dance from *Coppélia* we used dime-store fans to practice the arm movements.

There has been no attempt to analyze the music except to reduce it to the appropriate counts, which are usually in groups of eight. There are many rhythms used in ballet of which the waltz seems to be the most popular. Adaptations of folk dance rhythms used as the mazurka, polonaise, tarantella, bolero, galop, polka, gigue, and so forth are also used by composers, and in turn are used by the choreographers.

There are piano scores, which I refer to throughout the text, available for most of the classical ballets in which these variations appear. Having a pianist play for class is helpful, as the tempo can then be adjusted for the dancers. But because more and more teachers are using recordings because of the shortage of suitable pianists and the money to pay them, I have also tried to suggest recordings that I found most suitable to the dancing tempo. (Most of the music for the variations found in recordings of the ballets seems to be at a faster tempo than is comfortable, or humanly possible, to dance to.) One way to meet this problem is to obtain a variable-speed phonograph to slow down the tempo enough to dance to it and then, if desired, transfer the recording at a slower tempo to a tape via a reel tape recorder or a cassette tape recorder. A variable-speed cassette tape recorder can be found on the market.

The drawings in this book attempt to catch the essence of each variation, stimulate the imagination of the student, and illustrate the steps in appropriate costumes. Photographs of famous dancers in these ballets should also serve as inspiration.

The great choreographer Marius Petipa of the St. Petersburg Maryinsky Theatre has the greatest representation in this collection of variations. Of course, there are many more variations that have not yet been notated, as this is only a sampling.

The Russian, Italian, and French methods of teaching ballet each have different numbered positions for the arms. The Russian system, which is based on the French and Italian methods, was first clarified by Agrippina Vaganova at the Imperial Ballet School in St. Petersburg. Vaganova declared that the preparatory position plus three basic numbered positions are all that are necessary to describe the positions of the arms, and all the other classical positions of the arms can be derived from combinations of one arm in one of the basic positions with the other arm in another of the basic positions. Although the Russians later added three more numbered positions of the arms, the Vaganova method of numbering the arm positions is used in the notation in this book because it seems to be the simplest and least confusing.

In addition, the four numbered arabesque positions of the Russian method with corresponding arm positions are used in this notation; that is: arms in first arabesque position, arms in second arabesque position, arms in third arabesque position, and arms in fourth arabesque position. The position of the arms in third arabesque position is also used in the demi-plié preparation for pirouettes from fourth position croisé, as it gives a greater force for the turns when taking the preparation in this manner.

PREPARATORY POSITION OF THE ARMS

Arms are held in a low position in front of the body en bas on a level with the thighs, with elbows rounded and the palms of the hands curved and facing slightly upward and toward the body with the fingertips a few inches apart.

FIRST POSITION OF THE ARMS

Both arms are raised in front of the body en avant on a level with the stomach, with the elbows rounded and the hands curved so that the palms are facing the body. This is the gateway position through which the arms usually pass from one position to the other. A wide variation of this position with the arms opening slightly outward with the palms turned slightly upward is used as a final pose to indicate the giving of oneself to the audience.

SECOND POSITION OF THE ARMS

Both arms are raised to the sides slightly below shoulder level with the elbows slightly rounded and the palms curved facing front.

This is the standard à la seconde position, with a variation called demi-seconde or demi-hauteur in which the arms are halfway down between the line of the shoulders and the hips, which gives a softer quality. In second position allongé the arm is extended slightly higher than shoulder level with elbow straight and palm facing downward, usually in the écarté position of the body.

THIRD POSITION OF THE ARMS

Both arms are raised above the head en haut with the elbows rounded, the palms facing downward and the fingertips almost touching. The arms should be slightly in front of the body so that when looking up one can see the hands. This position becomes allongé when the arms are opened slightly outward, the elbows straightened, and the palms turned outward.

ARMS IN FIRST ARABESQUE POSITION

In first arabesque position the leg nearer to the audience is raised back at a right angle to the body, which is supported on one leg in profile to the audience. The arm on the same side as the supporting leg is extended forward on the same level as the eyes with the palm down and the wrist slightly curved. The other arm is extended back in second position slightly behind the line of the shoulder.

ARMS IN SECOND ARABESQUE POSITION

In second arabesque position, the body and legs are in the same position as for first arabesque but with the arm nearer to the audience extended forward and the arm on the same side as the supporting leg brought back of the line of the shoulder far enough so that it can be seen by the audience. Look toward the audience over the shoulder of the arm that is front.

ARMS IN THIRD ARABESQUE POSITION

In third arabesque position the body is facing croisé with the supporting leg nearer to the audience and the other leg raised back at a right angle to the body. The arm on the same side as the raised leg is extended forward while the other arm is extended to the side in second position. Look toward the arm which is in front.

In fourth arabesque position, the body and legs are in the same position as for third arabesque. The arm on the same side as the supporting leg is extended forward with the shoulder brought forward so that the back is half-turned toward the audience in an épaulé position; the other arm is brought back far enough so that it can be seen by the audience. Look toward the audience over the shoulder of the arm that is forward.

The following numbered diagram indicates the directions in which the body faces while performing the variations as described in the text. The numbers are consecutive in a clockwise direction, starting with 1 facing front toward the audience.

AUDIENCE

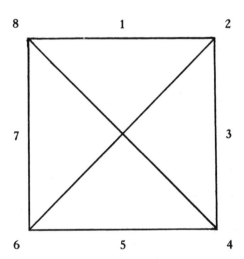

In the form of notation I have decided upon the French terminology to describe the step is stated first, with the detailed description of the movement following. This description together with the line drawings, the counts, and the floor patterns should help anyone who has a previous knowledge of ballet to correctly decipher the variations.

The French terms used in the text are derived from ballet dictionaries and encyclopedias of the dance. The three basic methods of ballet, i.e., French, Italian, and Russian sometimes use different

French terms to describe the same ballet step. For instance "pas de bourrée couru en cinquième" may be described by the term "pas suivi" and "pas de bourrée couru en première," by the term "pas couru," going from the French to the Russian method. One does not go into such detail in an actual ballet class, which relies less on terminology and more on demonstration and on simple key words such as relevé, bourrée, passé, plié, arabesque, and so forth. In this text I also use the term "sous-sus" to denote "relevé in fifth position in place" because Madame Shollar used it constantly in class, although it may be considered incorrect by some sources.

In conclusion, I can only express the hope that this book will record some of the grandeur of the great classical ballets of the past and will fill a need of teachers, students, and choreographers of the art of ballet by bringing the variations to life through these pages.

LAURENCIA KLAJA

Acknowledgments

From the many ballet teachers, both male and female, with whom I have studied and gained useful balletic knowledge, including the great Alexandra Danilova, whom I cherish, I wish to single out the late Ludmilla Shollar, to whom this book is dedicated; Anatole Vilzak, her husband; and the late Barbara Fallis, whose teachings are the backbone of this book.

My thanks to Selene Fung for her complete cooperation in expressing my ideas for the line drawings and diagrams; to Beverley Gallegos for her help and advice; and to Louise Gault, my editor, for her interest and understanding.

Special thanks to Penny Chrisman who helped in identifying the piano music.

The Dance of the Sugar Plum Fairy is a revised version of my notation of the *Sugar Plum Fairy Variation* that was published in the April 1979 issue of *Dance Magazine*.

Three descriptions of the variations of Princess Aurora, the Lilac Fairy, and the Silver Fairy from *The Sleeping Beauty* are excerpted from the *Borzoi Book of Ballets* by Grace Robert, published by Alfred A. Knopf, Inc., in 1946 and now out of print.

A Ballerina Prepares

CLASSICAL BALLET VARIATIONS
FOR THE FEMALE DANCER

SWANILDA'S VARIATION
TO A SLAVIC THEME

From the Ballet

Coppélia

ou La Fille aux Yeux d'Émail
[or The Girl with the Enamel Eyes]

Alexandra Danilova and Frederic Franklin
as Swanilda and Franz in COPPÉLIA.

SWANILDA'S VARIATION
TO A SLAVIC THEME

Prima ballerina variation for Swanilda from Act I of the ballet *Coppélia*. MUSIC by Léo Delibes. CHOREOGRAPHY probably by Marius Petipa and/or Lev Ivanov. AS TAUGHT by Ludmilla Shollar. NOTATED by Laurencia Klaja. TEMPO 2/4, un peu retenu.

Recommended Recording

Coppélia, Complete Ballet by Delibes. Conducted by Yuri Fayer, with the Bolshoi Theatre Orchestra. Melodiya/Angel Records, STEREO SRB 4111, side 1.

The adagio violin solo "Ballade de l'Épi" as a pas de deux for Swanilda and Franz depicting "The Legend of the Ear (of Corn)" precedes the "Thème Slave Varié," a divertissement that includes an Introduction, First Variation, Second Variation, Third Variation, Fourth Variation (Clarinet Solo), and Coda. This variation is the fourth selection, called Third Variation, and precedes the clarinet solo of the Fourth Variation.

Piano Music

Coppélia, Ballet Complet, by Léo Delibes. This variation is found in Act I on page 32, Third Variation of the "Thème Slave Varié." According to a footnote, the theme was extracted from the music "Échos de Pologne" (Echos of Poland), by the Polish composer Moniuszko. Published by Lyrebird Music Press.

Comments

The music is divided into an energetic masculine assertion alternating with a sprightly feminine response throughout the balletic combinations of this variation. The mood of this dance is gay and slightly mischievous. This is a variation for Swanilda as she dances with her friends in an Eastern European village square. Later, in the finale of this divertissement, a series of skimming brisés dessus downstage on a diagonal for Swanilda adds fire to the Coda. Alexandra Danilova was one of the greatest Swanildas of all time and this finale was one of the highlights of her performance.

The libretto is taken from a story by E. T. A. Hoffmann, "Der Sandmann." The story is about a doll called Coppélia, named after her creator, Dr. Coppélius, and the adventures of Swanilda, whose fiancé, Franz, falls in love with the life-sized doll, thinking it is the daughter of Dr. Coppélius.

The first production of *Coppélia, ou La Fille aux Yeux d'Émail* (or The Girl with the Enamel Eyes) premiered in Paris in 1870 with choreography by Arthur Saint-Léon, who died the same year. Marius Petipa choreographed the first Russian production in 1884.

INTRODUCTION*

Stand at center stage, facing the audience.

For an opening cue, use the ending of the prior music (if you are using a recording).

STAND WITH LEFT FOOT POINTE TENDUE CROISÉE FOURTH POSITION FRONT: Right arm is in first position front; left arm is in second position. Look toward the audience.

* *When counting the music for this variation, please note that the accent is usually down instead of up, a characteristic of Slavic folk dance.*

ONE

This combination moves to the right toward side 3.

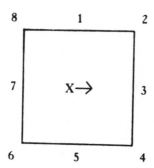

PAS DE CHAT—COUNT *one:*   Step forward transferring weight to left foot in demi-plié, at the same time raising right leg with the knee well bent. Jump upward off left foot bending the left knee; come down first on the right foot, then bring left foot to fifth position front demi-plié.

RELEVÉ WITH DÉVELOPPÉ À LA SECONDE—COUNT *and:*   Relevé quickly onto left pointe with a développé to second position en l'air écarté to corner 2 with right foot (90°). Right arm moves from first position to third position en haut while the left arm remains in second position. Look toward downstage right (corner 2).

DEMI-PLIÉ IN FIFTH POSITION—COUNT *two, and:*   The right leg closes quickly front in fifth position demi-plié. Right arm opens outward to second position; left arm remains in second position; then both move downward to low first position. Look toward corner 2.

RELEVÉ-RETIRÉ AND DEMI-PLIÉ IN FIFTH POSITION—COUNT *three:*   Relevé on left pointe bringing right foot retiré in front of the left knee. Right arm moves to first position en avant while left arm moves to second position. Look over right arm and elbow.

—Right leg closes quickly front in fifth position demi-plié. Right arm sways to left while remaining in first position front. Left arm also sways to the left, remaining in second position without twisting shoulders, to gain momentum for following pirouette(s). Look front toward audience.

Relevé with développé
à la seconde

PIROUETTE(S) EN DEHORS FROM FIFTH POSITION—COUNT *and:* Execute a single or double pirouette en dehors from fifth position rising on left pointe and bringing right foot retiré front of left knee. Force is given from left shoulder after right arm sways to right to give momentum and then both arms meet in first position en avant. Head spots front.

FINISH IN FIFTH POSITION AND STRAIGHTEN KNEES—COUNT *four, and:* After pirouette(s) close right foot back into fifth position demi-plié. Remaining in fifth position quickly straighten both knees, with both feet remaining flat on the floor. Arms open front between first and second positions with palms facing slightly upward extended toward the audience. Head inclines slightly to the right with a slightly mischievous smile on the face.

*Mary Jago and Rudolf Nureyev
as Swanilda and Franz in* COPPÉLIA.

TWO

This combination moves to center back while facing front.

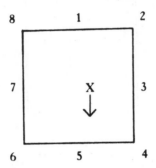

RELEVÉ PASSÉ WITH LEFT FOOT—COUNT *one:* Demi-plié in fifth position and relevé onto the right pointe while raising left foot retiré to front of right knee. With the accent down close left foot in fifth position back demi-plié. Left arm moves to first position en avant and executes a port-de-bras from first position outward to second position with the palm turning slightly outward. The right arm remains in second position. Head turns slightly to the left. The left shoulder moves slightly back with right shoulder front.

RELEVÉ PASSÉ WITH RIGHT FOOT—COUNT *two:* Relevé onto left pointe while raising right foot retiré to front of left knee and with the accent down, close right foot to fifth position back demi-plié. Right arm moves to first position en avant and executes a port-de-bras from first position outward to second position with the palm turning slightly outward while the left arm remains in second position. Head turns slightly to the right. The right shoulder moves slightly back with left shoulder front.

RELEVÉ PASSÉ WITH LEFT FOOT—COUNT *three:* Same as count *one.*

RELEVÉ PASSÉ WITH RIGHT FOOT—COUNT *four:* Same as count *two.*

THREE

This combination moves straight forward toward audience.

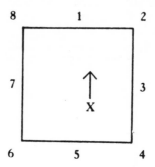

PAS DE BOURRÉE COURU IN FIRST POSITION—COUNT *five:* With a demi-plié on right leg step forward and piqué on left pointe toward the audience. Bourrée in first position in double time so that the accent is on the left foot moving front; that is: left foot sur la pointe, right foot sur la pointe. Arms open to and remain in second position. Body leans slightly forward with head also slightly forward; look downward.

PAS DE BOURRÉE COURU IN FIRST POSITION—COUNT *six:* Left foot, right foot. Body, head, and arms remain the same.

PAS DE BOURRÉE COURU IN FIRST POSITION—COUNT *seven, and:* Left foot, right foot, sur les pointes in first position, then move left foot in front of right foot into fifth position and demi-plié. Arms move downward to preparatory position. Body and head straighten.

FOUR

Repeat combination ONE exactly.

FIVE

Repeat combination TWO exactly.

SIX

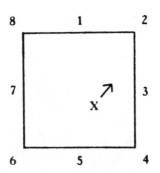

Repeat combination THREE but move forward toward corner 2 on a diagonal.

SEVEN

This combination moves toward side 7.

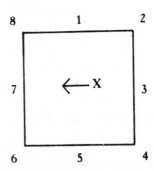

GLISSADE CHANGÉE TO LEFT—COUNT *one:* From fifth position with left foot in front, demi-plié and execute a quick glissade to the left (side 7), changing feet so that right foot comes fifth position front demi-plié. Arms open to low second position and then close to preparatory position. Body faces front as head turns slightly to the left.

Piqué à la seconde

PIQUÉ À LA SECONDE—COUNT *and:*   With a demi-plié on the right foot, dégagé the left foot toward side 7 and piqué onto the left pointe. At the same time raise right leg straight to second position in the air (90°) without développé. Arms open to second position from first position en avant. Body and head face front.

BALLONNÉ—COUNT *two, and:*   Remaining sur la pointe on left foot, bend the right knee and bring right foot retiré behind left knee; then demi-plié in fifth position with right foot back. The right arm moves upward to third position en haut from second position and left arm moves to first position en avant. Body inclines to the left side. Head is inclined and turned to the left side also. On demi-plié in fifth position, right arm moves straight down to meet left arm in first position en avant; the body and head straighten and face front.

GLISSADE CHANGÉE TO LEFT—COUNT *three:* Same as count *one.*

PIQUÉ À LA SECONDE; BALLONNÉ—COUNT *and, four, and:* Same as count *and, two, and.*

EIGHT

This combination remains in one spot (sur place).

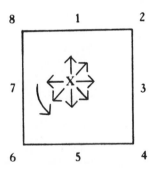

SEVEN RELEVÉS PASSÉS EN TOURNANT EN DEHORS—making one complete turn to the left.

RELEVÉ PASSÉ WITH LEFT FOOT CLOSING BACK—COUNT *one:* Relevé on right foot sur la pointe bringing left foot retiré to side of right knee. Immediately close back in fifth position demi-plié with the accent down, facing side 7. Left arm is in first position en avant with the right arm in second position. Body inclines slightly to the left. Look downward over left arm.

RELEVÉ PASSÉ WITH LEFT FOOT CLOSING FRONT—COUNT *two:* Relevé on right foot sur la pointe, bringing left foot retiré to side of right knee. Immediately close front in fifth position demi-plié with the accent down, facing corner 6. Arms, body, and head remain the same.

RELEVÉ PASSÉ WITH LEFT FOOT CLOSING BACK—COUNT *three:* Same as count *one* except the body faces side 5.

RELEVÉ PASSÉ WITH LEFT FOOT CLOSING FRONT—COUNT *four:* Same as count *two* except body faces corner 4.

RELEVÉ PASSÉ WITH LEFT FOOT CLOSING BACK—COUNT *five:* Same as count *one* except body faces side 3.

RELEVÉ PASSÉ WITH LEFT FOOT CLOSING FRONT—COUNT *six:* Same as count *two* except body faces corner 2.

RELEVÉ PASSÉ WITH LEFT FOOT CLOSING BACK—COUNT *seven, eight:* Same as count *one* except that body faces the audience.

NINE

This combination moves toward side 3.

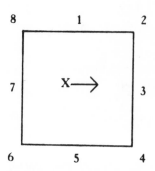

Repeat combination SEVEN to the opposite side.

Gelsey Kirkland and Mikhail Baryshnikov
as Swanilda and Franz in COPPÉLIA.

TEN

*This combination remains in place for three counts
and then moves toward corner 8.*

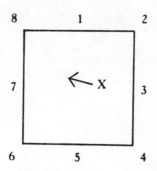

RELEVÉ PASSÉ WITH RIGHT FOOT CLOSING BACK—COUNT *one:* Remain facing front and relevé on left foot sur la pointe, bringing right foot retiré to side of left knee. Immediately close back in fifth position demi-plié with the accent down. The right arm is in first position front en avant and left arm is in second position. Body inclines slightly to the right. Look downward over right arm.

RELEVÉ PASSÉ WITH RIGHT FOOT CLOSING FRONT—COUNT *two:* Remain facing front and relevé on left foot sur la pointe, bringing right foot retiré to side of left knee. Immediately close front in fifth position demi-plié with the accent down. Arms, body, and head remain the same.

SOUS-SUS SUR LES POINTES—COUNT *three:* Relevé in place sur les pointes in fifth position changing épaulement to face corner 8. Bring left arm to first position en avant and right arm to second position. Body inclines slightly to the left. Look over the left arm.

RUN ON DEMI-POINTES TOWARD CORNER 8, RIGHT FOOT, LEFT FOOT, RIGHT FOOT, LEFT FOOT—COUNT *four, five, six, seven:* From sur les pointes fifth position step forward onto the demi-pointe of the right foot and run on demi-pointes. Arms open downward in low second position slightly back of the body. Body and head incline slightly forward; look downward.

—Step forward onto left foot. Arms, head, and body remain the same.

—Step forward onto right foot. Arms, head, and body remain the same.

—Step forward onto left foot into a demi-plié with a small dégagé front croisé with right foot.

ASSEMBLÉ FRONT CROISÉ—COUNT *eight:* With a small jump on left foot execute a small assemblé croisé front toward corner 8, with the right foot closing in fifth position front demi-plié. Arms are in preparatory position. Body and head straighten facing corner 8.

ELEVEN

This combination moves back and forth toward corner 6 and then toward corner 2 on a diagonal.

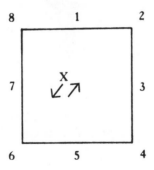

ENTRECHAT-CINQ—COUNT *one:* With a strong demi-plié in fifth position right foot front, jump into the air in place off both feet and execute an entrechat-cinq, which is similar to an entrechat-quatre but ends with left foot back sur le cou-de-pied with a strong demi-plié on right foot. Arms remain en bas in preparatory position. Body is straight with the right shoulder slightly forward, head is turned to the right shoulder to face corner 2.

PIQUÉ BACK RAISING RIGHT FOOT ÉCARTÉ À LA SECONDE—COUNT
and: Step back on left pointe to corner 6 and raise right foot
in écarté in second position en l'air (90°) to corner 2, without
développé. Arms move to first position front en avant with left
arm continuing en haut to third position and right arm opening
to second position. Body inclines slightly to the left. Head is
turned toward left arm.

DEMI-PLIÉ IN FIFTH POSITION EFFACÉ—COUNT *two:* Quickly close
right foot front in fifth position effacé demi-plié. The left arm
closes inward and downward to meet the right arm in front in
first position. Head faces front.

Sissonne sur les pointes
into penchée arabesque

SISSONNE SUR LES POINTES INTO PENCHÉE ARABESQUE—COUNT
and, three: From fifth position demi-plié spring into relevé onto
the right pointe, at the same time raising the left leg back into
effacée arabesque traveling slightly to corner 2. Lean forward
into penchée arabesque so that as the leg rises higher than 90°,
the head and body remain in the same line and move lower forward like a seesaw. Arms open into first arabesque position with
the right arm front. Look downward toward corner 2.

DEMI-PLIÉ FIFTH POSITION EFFACÉ—COUNT *and, four, and:* Close left foot back into fifth position effacé in demi-plié. Arms move downward to preparatory position en bas.

TWELVE

This combination remains in one spot sur place.

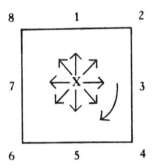

EIGHT ÉCHAPPÉS SUR LES POINTES EN TOURNANT EN DEHORS—making one complete turn to the right.

ÉCHAPPÉ SUR LES POINTES—COUNT *one:* Échappé sur les pointes into second position to face side 3 immediately closing right foot in fifth position *back* demi-plié with the accent down. Arms begin to move upward through first position en avant. Body is straight. Look slightly downward at arms.

ÉCHAPPÉ SUR LES POINTES—COUNT *two:* Échappé sur les pointes into second position to face corner 4, immediately closing right foot in fifth position *front* demi-plié with the accent down. Arms continue to move upward. Body is straight. Head follows the movement of the arms upward.

ÉCHAPPÉ SUR LES POINTES—COUNT *three:* Échappé sur les pointes into second position to face side 5, immediately closing right foot in fifth position *back* demi-plié with the accent down. Arms continue to move upward toward third position en haut. Body is straight. Look toward arms.

Échappé sur les pointes

ÉCHAPPÉ SUR LES POINTES—COUNT *four:* Échappé sur les pointes
into second position to face corner 6, immediately closing right
foot in fifth position *front* demi-plié with the accent down. Arms
are in third position en haut. Body is straight. Look upward toward arms.

ÉCHAPPÉ SUR LES POINTES—COUNT *five:* Échappé sur les pointes
into second position to face side 7, immediately closing right foot
in fifth position *back* demi-plié with the accent down. Arms
begin to open outward from third position en haut. Body is
straight. Head follows movement of the right arm.

ÉCHAPPÉ SUR LES POINTES—COUNT *six:* Échappé sur les pointes
into second position to face corner 8, immediately closing right
foot in fifth position *front* demi-plié with the accent down. Arms
continue to move outward toward second position. Body is
straight. Head follows movement of the right arm.

Échappé sur les pointes—count *seven:* Échappé sur les pointes into second position to face front to audience, immediately closing right foot in fifth position *back* demi-plié with the accent down. Arms are in second position. Body is straight. Look toward audience.

Échappé sur les pointes—count *eight:* Échappé sur les pointes into second position to face corner 2, immediately closing right foot in fifth position *front* demi-plié with the accent down, but with a stronger demi-plié as preparation for the following entrechat-cinq. Arms move downward to preparatory position. Body and head face corner 2.

THIRTEEN

This combination moves back and forth toward corner 6 and then toward corner 2 on a diagonal.

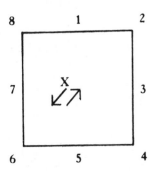

This combination is a partial repeat of combination ELEVEN.

Entrechat-cinq—count *one:* Same as combination ELEVEN—count *one.*

Piqué back raising right foot écarté à la seconde; demi-plié in fifth position effacé—count *and, two:* Same as combination ELEVEN—count *and, two, and.*

Sɪssᴏɴɴᴇ sᴜʀ ʟᴇs ᴘᴏɪɴᴛᴇs ɪɴᴛᴏ ᴘᴇɴᴄʜÉᴇ ᴀʀᴀʙᴇsQᴜᴇ—ᴄᴏᴜɴᴛ *and, three:* Same as *combination* ᴇʟᴇᴠᴇɴ—count *and, three.*

Dᴇᴍɪ-ᴘʟɪÉ ꜰɪꜰᴛʜ ᴘᴏsɪᴛɪᴏɴ ᴄʀᴏɪsÉ—ᴄᴏᴜɴᴛ *and:* Close left foot fifth position back croisé demi-plié. Arms move downward to preparatory position. Body and head face audience.

Sᴏᴜs-sᴜs sᴜʀ ʟᴇs ᴘᴏɪɴᴛᴇs—ᴄᴏᴜɴᴛ *four, and:* From demi-plié in fifth position with right foot in front, spring into fifth position sur les pointes croisé in place to corner 8. Arms pass through preparatory position to first position. The right arm remains in first position en avant and the left arm moves through first position into second position. Body faces front to audience with right shoulder slightly forward. Head is turned slightly to the right; look front toward audience.

FOURTEEN

This combination moves straight toward side 3 and then toward corner 2.

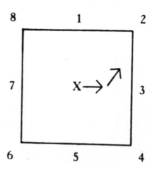

Fᴏᴜʀ ᴄʜᴀÎɴÉs-ᴅÉʙᴏᴜʟÉs ᴛᴏᴜʀs—ᴄᴏᴜɴᴛ *one* ᴛʜʀᴏᴜɢʜ *four:* From fifth position sur les pointes, dégagé right foot front éffacé to corner 2 with a demi-plié on left foot and execute four chaîné-déboulé turns sur les pointes in the direction of side 3. The right arm opens to second position; then both arms close to first position and remain there on the turns. Head spots to side 3.

STEP FORWARD ON RIGHT FOOT IN DEMI-PLIÉ—COUNT *five:* Coming down off pointe, step to right side on right foot with demi-plié toward corner 2. Arms open to second position. Look toward corner 2.

STEP FORWARD ON LEFT FOOT IN DEMI-PLIÉ—COUNT *six:* Coming down off pointe, step over in front of right foot to right side with demi-plié in fourth position toward corner 2. Arms close into first position en avant. Look toward corner 2.

PAS DE CHAT INTO POINTE TENDUE CROISÉE—COUNT *seven:* Lift the right foot sur le cou-de-pied back and spring into the air off the left foot. At the same time bend the left knee and move to the right toward corner 2. Come down on the right foot in demi-plié and then on the left foot front in fourth position demi-plié, immediately straightening the left knee, and pointe tendue croisée with right foot back. This is the final pose. Arms move through first position front to third position en haut while looking to the right to corner 2 during the pas de chat. On the pointe tendue the arms open outward to second position, with the right arm continuing the movement to extend front toward audience with the palm upward while the left arm remains in second position. Look toward audience.

THE DANCE OF
THE SUGAR PLUM FAIRY

From the Ballet

The Nutcracker

Casse Noisette

Patricia McBride and Jean-Pierre Bonnefous
as the Sugar Plum Fairy and her Cavalier in THE NUTCRACKER.

Nadezhda Pavlova and Vyacheslav Gordeyev
as Masha and the Prince in THE NUTCRACKER.

THE DANCE OF
THE SUGAR PLUM FAIRY

Prima ballerina variation from the Act II Pas de Deux of *The Nut-cracker* ballet. Music by Peter Ilyich Tchaikovsky. Choreography by Lev Ivanov. As taught by Ludmilla Shollar. Notated by Laurencia Klaja. Tempo 2/4, andante ma non troppo.

Recommended Recordings

1. *Nutcracker/Baryshnikov*. The American Ballet Theatre Production of Tchaikovsky's *Nutcracker*. The National Philharmonic Orchestra, conducted by Kenneth Schermerhorn. Columbia Masterworks, Columbia Records/CBS, m2 35189.

2. *The Nutcracker, highlights from the ballet*. Conducted by Gennadi Rozhdestvensky, with the Bolshoi Theatre Orchestra. Monitor Records, mcs 2104.

(In this recording the variation is followed by a coda, therefore the ending of the variation is one bar of music short, which must be compensated for in the choreography by omitting the pause pointe tendue right foot to second position à terre—count *six* in *combination* twelve, and going immediately into pas de bourrée piqué dessous.)

Piano Music

Casse-noisette, The Nutcracker, (Shchelkunchik is the Russian title.) Opus 71, piano score, arranged by Peter Ilyich Tchaikovsky, edited by Joseph Ortiz. Act II, No. 14, Pas de Deux, Variation 2 (pour la danseuse, "Danse de la Fée Dragée"), page 136. Published by Lyre-bird Music Press.

Comments

Tchaikovsky composed The Nutcracker ballet according to the directions given to him by Marius Petipa, long-time choreographer for the Maryinsky Imperial Ballet, but the actual choreography was done by Lev Ivanov, who took Petipa's place when Petipa became ill.

The "Dance of the Sugar Plum Fairy" was conceived with the special tone of the celesta in mind. This instrument, invented by Mustel in Paris, was a cross between a small piano and a glockenspiel and had never before been heard in Russia. The variation takes its mood, which is very dainty and sweet, from this instrument, and practicing it with a phonograph recording will be an advantage, as far as orchestral sound is concerned, and an inspiration as well. The traditional color of the tutu worn by the Sugar Plum Fairy is pink, which best conveys the candy-sweetness of the role.

It is said that the great impresario Serge Diaghilev substituted this variation for Aurora's variation in the final pas de deux of the last act in his production of The Sleeping Beauty, which was called "Aurora's Wedding." In the last years of the Ballet Russe de Monte Carlo, Alexandra Danilova and Nathalie Krassovska alternated in the role, dancing a variation that was almost identical to this one. Later, George Balanchine created his version of The Nutcracker ballet with new choreography for the Sugar Plum Fairy variation, which ended with a fast coda of turns traveling in a circle. Rudolf Nureyev's version of The Nutcracker, based on Alexander Gorsky's revision of Ivanov's choreography, also has different choreography for what has become Clara's or Masha's variation, while Mikhail Baryshnikov also omitted the role of the Sugar Plum Fairy from his version for American Ballet Theatre. So it would seem that the original version of the Sugar Plum Fairy variation is being performed less and less on the stage.

INTRODUCTION

The following steps move on a diagonal to center stage from corner 6.
The effect should be as if tiptoeing in.

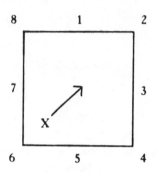

WAIT—COUNT *one, two:* Stand at corner 6. Wait two counts in
preparation with the right foot pointe tendue fourth position
front effacé with knees straight. The left hand holds edge of tutu
skirt; right arm is in second position. Body faces corner 2, head
looks left toward audience. (In a stage performance, the passés
développés may be started offstage in the wings on count *one,
two,* as in the following counts *three, four.*)

PASSÉ   DÉVELOPPÉ   EN   AVANT   CROISÉ   WITH   PIQUÉ—COUNT
three: Piqué onto the right pointe toward corner 2 as left leg
passes through retiré position at side of the right knee into
développé croisé front (45°). Demi-plié softly on the right leg
as left leg passes front croisé and left knee straightens. The left
hand holds edge of tutu skirt as before; right arm remains in second position. Head and body remain the same.

PASSÉ   DÉVELOPPÉ   EN   AVANT   EFFACÉ   WITH   PIQUÉ—COUNT
four: Same as count *three,* but done to the opposite side.
Arms remain same.

PASSÉ   DÉVELOPPÉ   EN   AVANT   CROISÉ   WITH   PIQUÉ—
COUNT *five:* Same as count *three,* but change hands so that
right hand holds the edge of the tutu skirt and left arm is in second position. Look toward corner 2. Body remains the same.

PASSÉ DÉVELOPPÉ EN AVANT EFFACÉ WITH PIQUÉ—COUNT *six:* Same as count *four,* but arms and head remain the same as for count *five.*

PASSÉ DÉVELOPPÉ EN AVANT CROISÉ WITH PIQUÉ—COUNT *seven:* Same as count *three,* but instead of demi-plié on the right leg, remain sur la pointe and hold balance with the left leg croisé front with straight knee (90°). The left leg points to corner 2. The right arm moves to third position en haut through first position en avant; left arm is in second position. Body remains the same. Look left toward audience.

TOMBÉ DESSUS—COUNT *eight:* Fall forward onto the left foot into demi-plié croisé bringing the right foot sur le cou-de-pied back as preparation for next combination. Open the right arm through second position to first position en avant; left arm remains in second position. Body remains facing corner 2. Look over the right arm.

ONE

This combination travels from side to side, starting to the right.

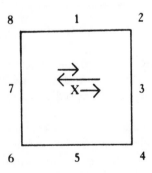

PAS DE BOURRÉE COURU EN PREMIÈRE SUR LES POINTES— COUNT *and:* Step to right on the right pointe and run quickly on the pointes toward side 3, right, left, right, left with tiny steps. Feet are in first position sur les pointes with knees slightly relaxed. The right arm is in first position en avant, the left arm is in second position. Body inclines slightly to the right; look over the right arm.

Pointe tendue effacée
à terre

POINTE TENDUE EFFACÉE À TERRE—COUNT *one:* Demi-plié on the
left leg and point right foot to fourth position front effacé on the
floor. Arms remain the same; body inclines right.

RELEVÉ WITH DOUBLE PETIT BATTEMENT BATTU FRONT—
COUNT *and:* Relevé on the left pointe simultaneously raising
right foot front en l'air (25°) and bringing it to sur le cou-de-
pied front. Beat the right foot twice front on left ankle. Arms
remain the same. The body straightens.

POINTE TENDUE EFFACÉE À TERRE—COUNT *two:* Come down on the
left leg in demi-plié with the right leg pointe tendue on the floor
in fourth position front effacé. Arms remain the same. The body
inclines to the right.

RELEVÉ INTO RETIRÉ FROM POINTE TENDUE—COUNT *and:* From pointe tendue position, relevé onto left pointe, at the same time lifting the right leg to retiré front of left knee. The right arm moves to front of chest with elbow bent and the hand held vertically under the chin, the palm facing toward the left. Left arm remains in second position. Body straightens; look front toward the audience.

DÉVELOPPÉ INTO SECOND ARABESQUE FONDUE CHANGING DIRECTION OF THE BODY—COUNT *three:* Continuing movement with momentum from previous relevé-retiré, turn body en dedans (toward the audience) to face side 7. At the same time développé right leg back into second arabesque and demi-plié on the left leg. The right hand continues movement from under chin position and pushes forward into second arabesque position while straightening the elbow. The left arm remains in second position. Look toward audience over the right shoulder.

PAS DE BOURRÉE CHANGÉE SUR LES DEMI-POINTES—COUNT *and, four:* Draw right foot under left foot rising sur les demi-pointes in fifth position with a passing movement and, remaining on the demi-pointes, step to second position à terre with left foot. Bring right foot in front of left foot in demi-plié as left foot is brought sur le cou-de-pied back. Arms move through second position on the pas de bourrée, ending with the left arm in first position en avant and the right arm in second position. Body faces corner 8 and inclines to the left side. Look over the left arm.

PAS DE BOURRÉE COURU EN PREMIÈRE SUR LES POINTES; POINTE TENDUE EFFACÉE À TERRE—COUNT *and, five:* Same as count *and, one,* but done to the opposite side.

RELEVÉ WITH DOUBLE PETIT BATTEMENT BATTU FRONT; POINTE TENDUE EFFACÉE À TERRE—COUNT *and, six:* Same as count *and, two,* but done to the opposite side.

RELEVÉ INTO RETIRÉ FROM POINTE TENDUE; DÉVELOPPÉ INTO SECOND ARABESQUE FONDUE CHANGING DIRECTION OF THE BODY—COUNT *and, seven:* Same as count *and, three,* but done to the opposite side.

PAS DE BOURRÉE CHANGÉE SUR LES DEMI-POINTES—COUNT *and, eight:* Same as count *and, four,* but done to the opposite side.

TWO

This combination moves diagonally backward to corner 6.

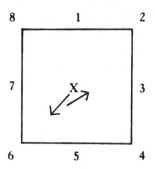

PETIT JETÉ DESSUS À CÔTÉ—COUNT *and:*   With a quick, sharp movement brush right leg to second position in the air (45°) and at the same time jump off the left foot. Come down with right foot front in demi-plié with the left foot sur le cou-de-pied back. The right arm closes first position en avant after opening in low second position on the spring into the air; the left arm remains in second position. Body straightens while in the air and inclines to right side again after alighting.

PIQUÉ EN ARRIÈRE WITH A DOUBLE PETIT BATTEMENT BATTU FRONT —COUNT *one:*   Piqué backward onto the left pointe to corner 6 and at the same time lift right foot to front of left ankle and execute a double battu front on the ankle. The left arm begins to move in to first position from second position; right arm remains in first position en avant. Body inclines slightly to the right side; look toward corner 2.

PETIT TOMBÉ FORWARD ONTO RIGHT FOOT—COUNT *and:*   Fall forward onto the right foot as the left foot comes sur le cou-de-pied back croisé. The left arm continues movement inward and is now in first position en avant, so that both arms are momentarily in first position. Body and head remain the same.

Piqué en arrière
with a double petit battement
battu front

PIQUÉ EN ARRIÈRE WITH A DOUBLE PETIT BATTEMENT BATTU FRONT
—COUNT *two:* Same as count *one* except arms are gradually
changing position. Left arm moves up to third position en haut
while the right arm remains in first position en avant. Body is
straight. Head remains the same.

PETIT TOMBÉ FORWARD ONTO RIGHT FOOT; PIQUÉ EN ARRIÈRE WITH A
DOUBLE PETIT BATTEMENT BATTU FRONT—COUNT *and,*
three: Same as count *and, two* except arms are gradually
changing position. The left arm moves straight downward from
third position en haut as the right arm remains in first position
en avant. Body and head remain the same.

Petit tombé forward onto right foot; piqué en arrière with a
 double petit battement battu front—count *and,
 four:* Same as count *and, two,* except arms continue to
 change position. As soon as arms meet in first position en avant,
 the right arm begins to move to third position en haut, and the
 left arm begins to open to second position. Body and head
 remain the same.

Piqué en arrière with a double petit battement battu front
 —count *and, five:* Same as count *one* for leg movements, but
 hold this count slightly longer. Arms have reached a position
 where the right arm is in third position en haut and the left arm
 is in second position. Body is straight; look front toward audience.

Tombé forward onto right foot, left foot dégagé back—
 count *six:* Fall forward onto right foot in demi-plié, at the
 same time extending left foot dégagé back with straight knee in
 low arabesque effacé. The right arm opens outward from third
 position en haut to second position with palm upward; left arm
 is in second position. Body and head incline to right side.

Pas de bourrée changée sur les demi-pointes—count *seven,
 and, eight:* The left foot steps in back of the right foot rising sur
 les demi-pointes in fifth position. Arms remain the same. Body
 faces front. Head looks toward corner 2.

—Remaining sur les demi-pointes, right foot opens to second position à terre. Arms are in low second position demi-hauteur.

—Bring the left foot in front of the right foot with demi-plié, at
 the same time bringing right foot pointe tendue croisée back.
 Straighten knees. The right arm moves to first position en avant;
 left arm remains in second position. Body faces corner 2; look toward the audience.

THREE

Repeat combination ONE exactly.

FOUR

This combination moves toward corner 4.

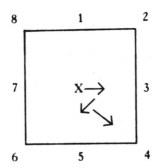

STEP ON RIGHT FOOT, STEP ON LEFT FOOT—COUNT *and, one:* Step
on right foot to side 3. Step on left foot over and in front of right
with a strong demi-plié as right foot moves to sur le cou-de-pied
back as preparation for arabesque. Both arms move to first position en avant. Body and head face side 3; look downward at the
arms.

PIQUÉ INTO SECOND ARABESQUE—COUNT *two:* Piqué onto the right
pointe to side 3 and raise left leg back in arabesque effacée. Both
arms open to second position; the left arm continues the movement moving downward, and with a sweeping motion it moves
forward into second arabesque position as right arm moves
slightly in back of shoulder line. Look over left shoulder toward
audience.

TOMBÉ FRONT AND STEP TO RIGHT CHANGING DIRECTION OF BODY—
COUNT *and, three:* Fall forward onto the left foot at the same
time changing direction of body to face corner 6; right foot is sur
le cou-de-pied back. Immediately step forward on the right foot
in demi-plié, at the same time bringing left foot sur le cou-de-
pied back facing side 7 as preparation for the next arabesque.
The left arm moves inward to meet right arm in first position en
avant. Body is facing side 7; look toward arms.

PIQUÉ INTO SECOND ARABESQUE—COUNT *four:* Piqué onto the left pointe to side 7 and raise right leg back in arabesque effacée. Both arms open to second position; the right arm continues the movement moving downward, and with a sweeping motion it moves forward into second arabesque position as the left arm moves slightly in back of shoulder line. Look over right shoulder toward the audience.

TOMBÉ BACK AND STEP TO LEFT CHANGING DIRECTION OF BODY—COUNT *and:* Tombé back onto the right foot at the same time changing direction of body to face corner 8. The left foot is extended front dégagé (25°) in écarté. Immediately step over on the left foot in demi-plié to face side 3, at the same time bringing the right foot sur le cou-de-pied back as preparation for next arabesque. The right arm moves inward to meet the left arm in first position en avant. Body is facing side 3; look toward arms.

PIQUÉ ARABESQUE WITH A HALF-TURN EN DEDANS—COUNT *five:* Piqué onto the right pointe to corner 4, executing a half-turn inward so that body finishes facing corner 8. Arms open to second position giving the impetus for the turn; the left arm continues the movement moving downward and with a sweeping motion moves forward into second arabesque position as the right arm moves slightly in back of shoulder line. Look over the left shoulder.

TOMBÉ BACK INTO FOURTH POSITION DEMI-PLIÉ AND POINTE TENDUE CROISÉE WITH RIGHT FOOT FRONT—COUNT *six:* From arabesque position fall back onto the left foot into fourth position croisé in demi-plié on both legs, facing corner 8. (Right foot is front.) Both arms move inward to first position en avant. Look toward the hands as body inclines slightly forward.

—Straighten both knees and pointe tendue right foot front croisé à terre. Body straightens; arms remain the same.

PORT-DE-BRAS MOVEMENT TO LEFT—COUNT *and, seven:* The left hand moves outward and front turning the palm of the hand slightly upward in wide first position. Body inclines to left; look toward the left hand.

PORT-DE-BRAS MOVEMENT TO RIGHT—COUNT *and, eight:* The right hand moves outward and front turning the palm of the hand slightly upward. Body inclines to the right; look toward the audience with a gracious expression.

FIVE

This combination moves on the diagonal from corner 4 toward corner 8.

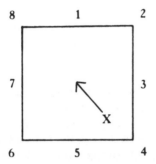

TOMBÉ EN AVANT—COUNT *and:* Transfer weight forward onto the right foot in demi-plié at the same time bringing the left foot sur le cou-de-pied back. Both arms close to first position en avant. Look toward hands.

TEMPS DE FLÈCHE—COUNT *one:* Brush left foot forward en l'air (25°) and immediately brush the right foot en l'air (45°) straight forward with knee straight. Jump up from the right foot so that the legs pass each other in the air, before alighting on the left foot in demi-plié with the right foot well extended dégagé front with straight knee (25°). Both arms move forward and upward with the left arm slightly higher. Palms face downward. Look toward the hands. Arms rise upward on the jump and come downward on the demi-plié, remaining extended front. The hands move downward as the arms move upward, and upward as the arms move downward. The head follows the movement of arms and hands. Body is facing corner 8.

DEMI-PLIÉ IN FIFTH POSITION—COUNT *and:* Quickly close the right foot front to demi-plié in fifth position croisé. Arms are in first position. Body is facing corner 8.

SOUS-SUS SUR LES POINTES—COUNT *two:* Spring onto the pointes drawing heels together into fifth position on the pointes (under-over) remaining sur place on relevé. Arms open to low second position with the hands at the edge of the tutu. Look toward the audience over the right shoulder. Body is facing corner 8.

TOMBÉ EN AVANT; TEMPS DE FLÈCHE—COUNT *and, three:* Same as count *and, one.*

DEMI-PLIÉ IN FIFTH POSITION; SOUS-SUS SUR LES POINTES—COUNT *and, four:* Same as count *and, two.*

PAS DE BOURRÉE SUR PLACE IN FIFTH POSITION—COUNT *and:* Remaining sur les pointes in fifth position, execute a fast bourrée in fifth position in place, transferring the weight front to the right foot and then back onto the left foot. Arms remain the same. Head inclines slightly to the right; look toward the audience.

RETIRÉ DERRIÈRE WITH LEFT FOOT—COUNT *five:* Transfer weight forward to right pointe at the same time raising the left foot to the back of right knee. Both arms move to the right side; left arm is across front of body with right arm in low second position with palms opening upward toward the audience. Head inclines toward right shoulder; look downward.

PAS DE BOURRÉE SUR PLACE IN FIFTH POSITION—COUNT *and:* Remaining sur la pointe on right foot, close left foot back in fifth position sur les pointes and execute a fast bourrée in fifth position in place transferring the weight back to the left foot and then front onto the right foot. Both arms are in low second position. Head is straight; look toward the audience.

RETIRÉ DEVANT WITH RIGHT FOOT—COUNT *six:* Transfer weight back to the left pointe and raise the right foot to front of the left knee. Both arms move to the left side; the right arm is across front of body with left arm in low second position, palms opening upward away from the audience. Head inclines slightly to the left shoulder; look downward.

RETIRÉ DERRIÈRE WITH LEFT FOOT—COUNT *and, seven:* Step in fifth position sur les pointes and, remaining sur la pointe on the right foot, raise the left foot to back of the right knee. Arms open to low second position. Head and body straighten.

RETIRÉ DEVANT WITH RIGHT FOOT—COUNT *and:* Step in fifth position sur les pointes and, remaining sur la pointe on left foot, raise the right foot to the front of left knee. Arms, head, and body remain the same.

CLOSE TO FIFTH POSITION SUR LES POINTES—COUNT *eight:* Remaining sur la pointe on the left foot, return the right foot to fifth position front sur les pointes. Arms, head, and body remain the same.

SIX

This combination moves on the diagonal to corner 8.

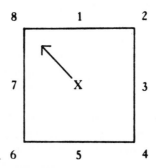

CONTINUING ON THE DIAGONAL, STEP FORWARD INTO DEMI-PLIÉ ON RIGHT FOOT WITH LEFT FOOT SUR LE COU-DE-PIED BACK. Repeat combination FIVE exactly, except on count *eight* close in fifth position demi-plié instead of sur les pointes.

SEVEN

This combination travels to side 3 in a slightly abrupt manner.

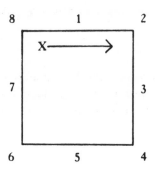

GLISSADE PRESSÉE DESSOUS CHANGÉE—COUNT *and:* Glissade in
double time to side 3 with a short step, changing the right foot to
fifth position back demi-plié. The right arm is in first position en
avant and left arm is in second position. Body faces front with
head slightly turned to the right.

PIQUÉ IN FIRST ARABESQUE—COUNT *one:* Quickly raise the right
foot sur le cou-de-pied back, at the same time turning body to
face side 3, and step into piqué on the right pointe and raise left
leg back into first arabesque. Arms move through first position
en avant to first arabesque position with right arm front. Body
is facing side 3 with head in profile to the audience.

ROTATION TO À LA SECONDE EN L'AIR WITH RETIRÉ—COUNT
and: Remaining sur la pointe on the right leg, quickly turn
the body to left so that the left leg rotates in the hip joint into
second position in the air, simultaneously bending the left knee
and bringing left foot to the front of the right knee. The right
arm moves quickly upward from arabesque position to third position en haut, while the left arm moves to first position en avant.
Body inclines slightly to the left side while facing front. Head
turns to left; look over the left arm.

Rotation to à la seconde
en l'air with retiré

DEMI-PLIÉ IN FIFTH POSITION WITH LEFT FOOT FRONT—COUNT
two: The left foot closes front in fifth position demi-plié facing front en face. The right arm moves downward to first position en avant to meet left arm, which is already in first position
en avant. Body straightens as head faces front.

GLISSADE PRESSÉE DERRIÈRE (NO CHANGE)—COUNT *and:* Glissade
in double time to side 3 without changing feet, so that right foot
closes fifth position back demi-plié.

PIQUÉ IN FIRST ARABESQUE—COUNT *three:* Same as count *one.*

ROTATION TO À LA SECONDE EN L'AIR WITH RETIRÉ; DEMI-PLIÉ IN
FIFTH POSITION WITH LEFT FOOT FRONT—COUNT *and,*
four: Same as count *and, two.*

GLISSADE PRESSÉE DERRIÈRE (NO CHANGE); PIQUÉ IN FIRST ARABESQUE—COUNT *and, five:* Same as count *and, three.*

ROTATION TO À LA SECONDE EN L'AIR WITH RETIRÉ; DEMI-PLIÉ IN FIFTH POSITION WITH LEFT FOOT FRONT—COUNT *and, six:* Same as count *and, two.*

GLISSADE PRESSÉE DERRIÈRE (NO CHANGE); PIQUÉ IN FIRST ARABESQUE—COUNT *and, seven:* Same as count *and, three.*

ROTATION TO À LA SECONDE EN L'AIR WITH RETIRÉ; DEMI-PLIÉ IN FIFTH POSITION WITH LEFT FOOT FRONT—COUNT *and, eight:* Same as count *and, two.*

EIGHT

This combination moves on a diagonal from corner 2 to center stage in a slow tempo.

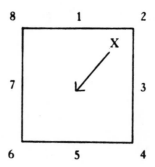

RELEVÉ PASSÉ WITH LEFT LEG—COUNT *and, one:* Relevé on right pointe as left leg rises to retiré to side of right knee, closing back in fifth position demi-plié. Left arm moves to third position en haut passing through first position as right arm moves to second position. Body inclines left with right shoulder slightly forward; look to corner 8. (The working leg and working arm are on the same side.)

Relevé passé with right leg

RELEVÉ PASSÉ WITH RIGHT LEG—COUNT *and, two:* Relevé on left
pointe as right leg raises to retiré to side of left knee, closing back
in fifth position demi-plié. The right arm moves to third position
en haut passing through first position as left arm moves to second
position. Body inclines right with left shoulder slightly forward;
look to corner 2.

RELEVÉ PASSÉ WITH LEFT LEG—COUNT *and, three:* Same as count
and, one.

RELEVÉ PASSÉ WITH RIGHT LEG—COUNT *and, four:* Same as count
and, two.

RELEVÉ PASSÉ WITH LEFT LEG—COUNT *and, five:* Same as count
and, one, except instead of closing the left leg into fifth position
demi-plié, bring the left foot sur le cou-de-pied back croisé with
demi-plié on the right leg. The left arm opens outward to second

position as right arm moves to first position en avant. Body inclines to right side with right shoulder forward. Look over the right arm.

GLISSADE BACK SUR LES POINTES—COUNT *and, six:* Piqué back onto left pointe toward corner 6 and draw the right foot front to fifth position sur les pointes. Arms remain the same. Body straightens and faces front en face. Look right toward corner 2.

PAS DE BOURRÉE COURU EN ARRIÈRE IN FIFTH POSITION—COUNT *and, seven:* (This movement is very slow and drawn out.) With tiny steps sur les pointes in fifth position with right foot front and the left leg leading, move backward on a diagonal until center of stage is reached. Both arms move together in a circular motion toward the left until they reach third position en haut with the arms in a rounded position over the head. Body faces front; look toward corner 2. (Pas de bourrée en tournant sur place to the right until the end of the count.)

HOLD FIFTH POSITION SUR LES POINTES—COUNT *and, eight:* Hold fifth position with right foot front croisé. Arms remain in third position en haut. Body faces front with right shoulder slightly forward. Head is slightly inclined to the right; look toward the audience.

NINE

This combination moves from side to side at center stage.

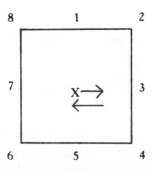

PAS DE CHAT RENVERSÉ WITH A QUARTER TURN TO RIGHT—COUNT

and, one: Demi-plié in fifth position and execute a quick small pas de chat by raising the right foot sur le cou-de-pied front and jumping up off left foot, at the same time changing direction of body away from audience in a quarter turn to face side 3. While still in the air, left foot passes sur le cou-de-pied front before alighting in fifth position demi-plié with left foot front. Both arms move outward to second position. Body inclines slightly to the left with the left shoulder forward. Head is slightly inclined over the left shoulder; look toward the audience.

DÉTOURNÉ SUR LES POINTES—COUNT *and, two:* Spring onto both pointes in fifth position while turning away from audience toward the foot that is back, so that the right foot forcefully moves front in fifth position sur les pointes to complete the three-quarters of the turn to again face the audience. While holding fifth position sur les pointes, the right hand moves from second position toward the body. Bend the elbow so that the palm is held gracefully under the chin in a vertical position with the palm facing toward the left. Left arm remains in second position. Look toward the audience.

PAS DE CHAT RENVERSÉ WITH A QUARTER TURN TO RIGHT—COUNT *and, three:* Same as count *and, one,* except that both arms move upward through first position en avant to third position en haut before opening outward to second position.

DÉTOURNÉ SUR LES POINTES—COUNT *and, four:* Same as count *and, two.*

PAS DE CHAT RENVERSÉ WITH A QUARTER TURN TO RIGHT—COUNT *and, five:* Same as count *and, three.*

DÉTOURNÉ SUR LES POINTES—COUNT *and, six:* Same as count *and, two.*

PIQUÉ IN FIRST ARABESQUE—COUNT *seven:* Demi-plié on right foot and raise left foot sur le cou-de-pied back while turning body to face side 7. Piqué onto left foot into first arabesque, raising right leg back. Arms move through first position en avant to first arabesque position, with left arm extended front. Head is in profile to audience; look toward the left wrist.

FONDU ON LEFT LEG, PAS DE BOURRÉE CHANGÉE—COUNT *and, eight:* Come down in demi-plié on left leg with right leg still extended back. Draw the right foot sur la pointe behind the left foot, rising sur les pointes in fifth position. Step to second position on left pointe and bring right foot front sur les pointes in fifth position croisé. Right hand moves toward the body while bending elbow so that the palm is held gracefully under the chin in a vertical position with the palm facing toward the left. Left arm is in second position. Body and head face the audience.

TEN

Repeat combination NINE exactly.

ELEVEN

This combination moves from side to side at center stage.

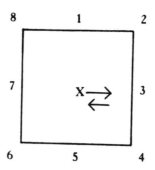

Repeat combination NINE up through count *seven*. Continue as follows:

FONDU IN FIRST ARABESQUE—COUNT *and, eight:* After the piqué arabesque, demi-plié on the left leg, raising right leg, which is already in arabesque, a little higher. Arms are in first arabesque position, with the left arm extended front. Body and head are facing side 7.

TWELVE

This combination moves from side to side and then forward at center stage.

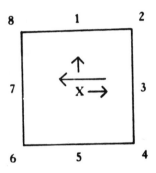

GLISSADE DERRIÈRE—COUNT *and:* Glissade to the right (side 3) without changing feet, commencing with the right foot dégagé to the side and closing the left foot fifth position front demi-plié. Arms move to first position en avant. Body faces front to audience with head turned slightly to the right.

PIQUÉ ARABESQUE—COUNT *one, two:* While turning the body to face side 3, demi-plié on the left foot and raise the right foot sur le cou-de-pied back. Piqué onto the right pointe and raise left foot back in first arabesque position. Right hand moves toward the lips and opens forward as if blowing a kiss toward side 3. The left arm is in second position, slightly back of shoulder line. Body is facing side 3, with the head in profile to the audience, chin raised slightly.

GLISSADE DERRIÈRE; PIQUÉ ARABESQUE—COUNT *and, three, four:* Same as count *and, one, two.*

FONDU CHANGING TO À LA SECONDE EN L'AIR (25°)—COUNT *and:* Demi-plié on the left leg with right leg dégagé back and quickly face front as the right leg rotates in the socket of the hip joint to low second position in the air. Arms are in low second position. Body and head face the audience.

PAS DE BOURRÉE COURU EN PREMIÈRE EN AVANT, RIGHT FOOT FORWARD, LEFT FOOT FORWARD, RIGHT FOOT FORWARD—COUNT *five:* In double time run forward in first position sur les pointes, commencing with a piqué forward onto the right pointe and continuing with three tiny steps toward the audience. (Legs are not turned out.) Arms remain in low second position. Body is inclined slightly forward; look downward. (Three emboîtés sur les pointes may be substituted for the bourrées.)

POINTE TENDUE RIGHT FOOT TO SECOND POSITION À TERRE—COUNT *six:* Step forward onto the left foot in demi-plié at the same time bringing the right foot to pointe tendue to the side on the floor. The right arm moves to first position en avant; left arm remains in second position. Body inclines to the right side; look toward the right foot.

PAS DE BOURRÉE PIQUÉ DESSOUS—COUNT *and seven, and eight:* Remaining in demi-plié on the left leg, raise the right leg off the floor (25°) in a low second position in the air. The right arm is in first position en avant and the left arm in second. Body is inclined to the right side; look toward the right foot as before.

—Step on the right pointe behind the left foot in fifth position and raise the left foot to retiré in front of the right knee. The left arm moves toward the body while bending the elbow so that the palm is held gracefully under the chin in a vertical position with the palm facing right. The right arm moves to second position. Body straightens; look slightly left toward corner 2.

—Remaining sur la pointe on the right foot, move left foot to a small second position sur les pointes, immediately raising the right foot retiré to the front of left knee. The left arm moves outward toward second position, while right arm begins to bend at elbow. Body and head face front to audience.

—Remaining sur la pointe on left foot, close the right foot front fifth position croisé sur les pointes and immediately raise the left foot retiré to the back of right knee. The right arm bends at the elbow while the right hand moves toward the body so that the palm is held gracefully under the chin in a vertical position with the palm facing left. Left arm is in second position. Body is slightly croisé to corner 8; look to the right toward audience.

Fifth position
sur les pointes

FIFTH POSITION SUR LES POINTES—COUNT *and:* Remaining sur la pointe on right foot, return left foot to fifth position back sur les pointes and hold final pose. Arms, body, and head remain the same.

RAYMONDA'S SCARF VARIATION

From the Ballet

Raymonda

Cynthia Gregory
and Rudolf Nureyev
as Raymonda
and Jean de Brienne
in RAYMONDA.

RAYMONDA'S
SCARF VARIATION

Prima ballerina variation from Act I of the ballet *Raymonda*. MUSIC by Alexander Glazunov. CHOREOGRAPHY by Marius Petipa. AS TAUGHT by Ludmilla Shollar. NOTATED by Laurencia Klaja. TEMPO 2/4, allegretto.

Recommended Recording

Raymonda Suite by Alexander Glazunov. Conducted by Yevgeny Svetlanov, with the Bolshoi Theatre Orchestra. Angel Melodiya SR-40172, side 1, Act I.

This variation is called "Prelude and Variation" and follows immediately after "Prelude and Romanesca." ("Raymonda's Scarf Variation" is sung by the voice of the solo harp.

Piano Music

Raymonda, Ballet in three acts by Alexander Glazunov. Edition of M. P. Belaieff. CAT NO. BEL-317. Sole agents: C. F. Peters Corp., 373 Park Avenue, New York, N.Y. 10016. Act I, page 38, "Prélude et Variation."

Follows immediately after "Prélude et Romanesca." "Raymonda passe son luth à une de ses compagnes et vient montrer une variante" are the stage directions written on the piano score.

Comments

Raymonda was first produced at the Maryinsky Theatre in St. Petersburg, Russia, on January 19, 1898, with choreography by Marius Petipa, and a libretto by Lydia Pashkova and Marius Petipa.

When learning this variation, notice how the unusual choreography is almost like the rhythms of a poem in the way the steps are repeated; a new ending added; a new set of steps introduced; a repetition; again a new ending, et cetera, all the while requiring the dexterous use of the scarf.

In Act I of Rudolf Nureyev's version, Raymonda, a young noblewoman of the Romanesque period of the middle ages (a period of valiant knights and gracious ladies) is being visited at her ancestral castle by her betrothed, the knight Count Jean de Brienne, who is going off on a crusade against the Saracens. Raymonda has been playing a lyre for her friends and her fiancé. She now gives the lyre to one of her friends and, taking a scarf that has been draped around her shoulders, proceeds to dance playfully with it.

INTRODUCTION

Stand at center stage.

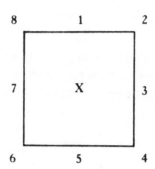

For an opening cue, use the ending of the harp solo, the "Prelude."

STAND IN FIFTH POSITION with left foot front facing en face to the audience. The arms are in second position with the right hand holding the scarf slightly forward. (The scarf should be of very soft material, such as silk, and at least a yard long and about a foot wide.)

ONE

This combination moves slightly to the right and then to the left toward side 7.

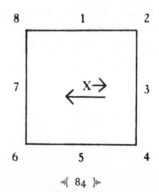

RELEVÉ-DÉVELOPPÉ À LA SECONDE—COUNT *one:* Demi-plié and, bringing the right foot to sur le cou-de-pied back, relevé on the left pointe sur place. At the same time développé the right leg to second position in the air (90°). Both arms raise slightly in second position so as to give impetus to the relevé-développé. Then move through preparatory position before passing upward through first position en avant to third position en haut. Body faces front; look toward corner 2.

DEMI-FOUETTÉ EN DEHORS INTO ARABESQUE FONDUE—COUNT *two:* Remaining sur la pointe on the left foot, and allowing the right leg to turn on the pivot of the right hip, turn into arabesque to the left, face side 7. Come down into a fondu (demi-plié) on the left foot. The right leg is extended back in arabesque position effacé. Arms open outward from third position en haut to second position; then right arm passes in front of body to extend to the left side so that both arms are in front of the body with the left arm slightly higher. The palms of both hands turn downward. The scarf follows the movement of the right arm, which gives it an extra flourish with the right wrist. Look toward side 7.

PAS DE BOURRÉE PIQUÉ—COUNT *three, and four:* Draw right foot behind left foot into fifth position sur les pointes. The right arm opens to demi-seconde position; left arm is in demi-seconde position. Head inclines to left.

—Remaining sur la pointe on the right foot, raise the left foot retiré to front of the right knee, and immediately step to second position à terre remaining sur les pointes. Arms remain demi-seconde. Look toward corner 8.

—Remaining sur la pointe on the left foot, raise right foot retiré to front of left knee and immediately close to fifth position front demi-plié en face. The right arm moves to first position front en avant; left arm is in second position. Look front.

TWO

This combination moves to the right toward side 3.

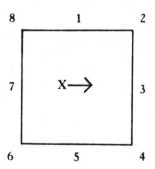

EMBOÎTÉ EN TOURNANT SUR LES POINTES—COUNT *one, and
two:* Relevé on right pointe, at the same time spring toward
the right and bring the left foot retiré front. Turn to the right to
face side 5. Immediately close the left foot front in fifth position sur les pointes. The right arm opens to second position as left
arm moves inward to first position front en avant to give impetus
to the turn. Look over left shoulder toward side 3.

—Remaining sur les pointes, pivot to the right again and bring
the right foot retiré front, so that body again faces front. Arms
change position so that the right arm moves inward to first position en avant and the left arm moves outward to second position.
Head spots to side 3.

—From retiré position with the right foot in front of the left knee,
and sur la pointe on the left foot, close to fifth position right foot
front effacé demi-plié. The right arm is in first position en avant
while the left arm is in second position. Look toward side 3.

EMBOÎTÉ EN TOURNANT SUR LES POINTES—COUNT *three, and
four:* Same as count *one, and two,* except last demi-plié in

fifth position with right foot front changes direction to croisé toward corner 8.

RELEVÉ DEVANT SUR LA POINTE—COUNT *and, five:* From demi-plié fifth position, relevé onto the left pointe bringing the right foot retiré front of the left knee. The right arm remains in first position en avant and the left arm remains in second position. Body is straight; look toward corner 8.

—Quickly, with a slight spring, return the right foot to fifth position front demi-plié croisé in preparation for the following pirouette. Arms remain the same.

SINGLE OR DOUBLE PIROUETTE EN DEHORS FROM FIFTH POSITION TO FIFTH POSITION—COUNT *six:* With a relevé onto the left pointe and bringing the right foot retiré to front of the left knee, execute a single or double pirouette en dehors to the right. Force for the pirouette is taken from the left shoulder as both arms sway slightly to the left and then to the right. Both arms meet in first position en avant during the turn. Head spots over left shoulder to corner 8. (Scarf should float around the body during the pirouette.)

FIFTH POSITION DEMI-PLIÉ AND STRAIGHTEN KNEES—COUNT *and, seven:* After the pirouette, close the right foot fifth position back demi-plié facing front and straighten knees. The right arm extends forward toward corner 2 and gracefully flourishes the scarf outward and forward with a movement of the wrist. The left arm opens to second position. Look toward the scarf.

THREE

Repeat combination ONE exactly.

FOUR

This combination moves toward corner 2.

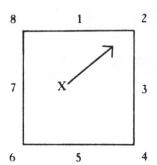

DÉGAGÉ FRONT EFFACÉ—COUNT *one:* With a demi-plié on the left foot, extend the right foot dégagé front slightly above the floor with a straight knee to effacé position toward corner 2. The right arm is forward holding the scarf; left arm is in second position. Body and head face corner 2.

GLISSADE EN AVANT EFFACÉ TO FIFTH POSITION SUR LES POINTES—COUNT *and, two:* Piqué forward onto the right pointe drawing the left foot behind right foot into fifth position sur les pointes effacé to corner 2. Hold this position while the right arm, which is forward holding the scarf, gives a flourish to the scarf with a movement of the wrist; left arm remains in second position. Look toward the scarf.

DÉGAGÉ FRONT EFFACÉ—COUNT *three:* Same as count *one.*

GLISSADE EN AVANT EFFACÉ TO FIFTH POSITION SUR LES POINTES—COUNT *and, four:* Same as count *and, two.*

WALK FORWARD SUR LES POINTES, RIGHT FOOT, LEFT FOOT, RIGHT FOOT, LEFT FOOT, AND PIQUÉ INTO FIRST ARABESQUE—COUNT *and, five, six, and, seven:* Remaining sur les pointes, step forward on the right leg toward corner 2 with knees slightly relaxed. Arms are in demi-seconde position. Body and head incline slightly forward. (Legs are not turned out.)

*Walk forward sur les pointes
and piqué into
first arabesque*

—Remaining sur les pointes, step forward on the left leg to corner 2 with knees slightly relaxed. Arms, body, and head remain the same.

—Remaining sur les pointes, step forward on the right leg to corner 2 with knees slightly relaxed. Arms, body, and head remain the same.

—Remaining sur les pointes, step forward on the left leg and quickly fondu into demi-plié on the left leg, at the same time bringing the right leg sur le cou-de-pied back. Arms move downward to preparatory position. Body straightens.

—Piqué onto the right pointe toward corner 2 and raise the left leg back into first arabesque effacée. On the arabesque, the right arm gives a flourish to the scarf forward toward corner 2; the left arm is in second position slightly back of shoulder line. Look toward the scarf.

FIVE

*This combination moves diagonally back toward corner 6, then
across to the right (side 3).*

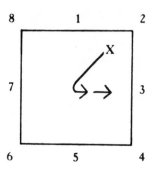

GLISSADE BACK WITH A HALF-TURN—COUNT *one:* From arabesque
  effacée position, fondu into demi-plié on the right foot with left
  leg dégagé back, and execute a glissade back with a half-turn to
  corner 6. Finish facing side 5 with left foot front in fifth position
  demi-plié. Arms move downward to preparatory position. Body
  is straight; head faces side 5.

BRISÉ DESSUS WITH HALF-TURN—COUNT *two:* Step forward on left
  foot to side 3 in demi-plié and brush right leg to low à la seconde
  en l'air, at the same time springing off the left foot and changing
  the direction of the body to the left with a half-turn so that the
  body faces front. Then bring the left foot behind the right calf
  and beat the two calves together before landing in fifth position
  demi-plié en face, with right foot back. Arms move upward
  through first position front en avant; the right arm, with the
  scarf, moves upward above shoulder level in second position
  allongé, and the left arm opens to the side in second position on
  a line with right arm but lower than shoulder level. Head is
  turned to the right; look toward the scarf.

GLISSADE TO RIGHT—COUNT *three:* With a dégagé of the right foot to second position à terre, glissade to the right to side 3 and close left foot fifth position front demi-plié (no change). Arms lower to preparatory position. Look right toward side 3.

ENTRECHAT-SIX DE VOLÉE—COUNT *and, four:** With the momentum gained from the preceding glissade, thrust the right leg to a low second position en l'air and, traveling to the right side (side 3), from demi-plié strongly bring the left calf behind the right calf and beat both calves together. Then change the position of legs en l'air so that the left leg is front and beat both calves together, coming down quickly into fifth position demi-plié with right foot front croisé.

SIX

This combination moves backward toward side 7.

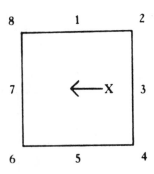

FIRST ARABESQUE WITH FONDU—COUNT *five:* Turning body slightly to the right (side 3), dégagé the right foot front and quickly step on the right foot. Raise the left leg back in first arabesque, and immediately fondu (demi-plié) on right foot with left leg dégagé back in first arabesque, body facing side 3. Arms open to first arabesque position with right arm holding the scarf in front. Look toward the scarf.

* *For an alternative version, see notes following this variation.*

A<small>RABESQUE</small> <small>VOYAGÉE</small>—<small>COUNT</small> *and six, and seven, and eight* (<small>COUNT</small> *eight* <small>IS SUSTAINED</small>):   Holding the left leg in first arabesque position and facing side 3, travel backward to side 7 with a series of six small jumps in demi-plié on the flat of the right foot. On the last count, raise the left leg slightly and hold position with demi-plié on the right leg. Arms are in high first arabesque position with the right arm front. The right arm lowers very gradually, at the same time flicking the scarf with the right wrist to get an undulating effect. Body lowers slightly during the voyagé. Look toward the scarf.

SEVEN

Repeat combination F<small>IVE</small> exactly.

EIGHT

This combination moves toward corner 2.

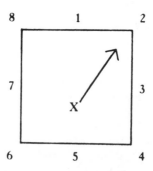

D<small>ÉGAGÉ</small> <small>FRONT</small> <small>EFFACÉ</small>; <small>GLISSADE</small> <small>EN</small> <small>AVANT</small> <small>EFFACÉ</small> <small>TO</small> <small>FIFTH</small> <small>PO-SITION</small> <small>SUR</small> <small>LES</small> <small>POINTES</small>—<small>COUNT</small> *and, five:*   Same as combination F<small>OUR</small>—count *one, and two,* but done in double time.

D<small>ÉGAGÉ</small> <small>FRONT</small> <small>EFFACÉ</small>; <small>GLISSADE</small> <small>EN</small> <small>AVANT</small> <small>EFFACÉ</small> <small>TO</small> <small>FIFTH</small> <small>PO-SITION</small> <small>SUR</small> <small>LES</small> <small>POINTES</small>—<small>COUNT</small> *and, six:*   Same as count *and, five.*

*Walk forward sur les pointes
and piqué into fourth arabesque*

WALK FORWARD SUR LES POINTES, RIGHT FOOT, LEFT FOOT, RIGHT
FOOT, AND PIQUÉ INTO FOURTH ARABESQUE—COUNT *and seven,
and eight:* Remaining sur les pointes, step forward on the right
leg toward corner 2 with knees slightly relaxed. Arms are in
demi-seconde position. Body and head incline slightly forward.
(Legs are not turned out.)

—Remaining sur les pointes, step forward on the left leg toward
corner 2 with knees slightly relaxed. Arms, body, and head
remain the same.

—Remaining sur les pointes, step forward on the right leg to
corner 2 with knees slightly relaxed and quickly fondu into demi-
plié on the right leg, at the same time bringing the left leg sur le
cou-de-pied back. Arms move downward to preparatory position.
Body straightens. Body and head face corner 2.

—Piqué onto the left pointe toward corner 2 and raise the right
leg back into fourth arabesque croisée. Arms move to fourth
arabesque position with the left arm front and the right arm
back. Head is épaulé over the left shoulder. Scarf is now behind
the body, in the right hand, as before.

NINE

This combination moves in a circular manner away from the audience and then returns to corner 2.

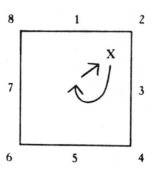

GLISSADE BACK WITH A HALF-TURN—COUNT *one:* Fondu into a demi-plié on the left foot with right foot dégagé back. Glissade back with a half-turn to the right to face back, closing left foot to fifth position front demi-plié. Arms move downward to preparatory position. Head turns toward right shoulder.

SAUTÉ À LA SECONDE EN TOURNANT—COUNT *two:* Step out on right foot to right side in demi-plié (still facing back), and brush left leg to à la seconde en l'air. With a strong jump off the right foot, turn the body to face front to the audience. Come down in demi-plié on the right foot with left leg extended à la seconde en l'air (90°). Both arms rise to third position en haut and open outward to second position. Look toward the audience.

ASSEMBLÉ SOUTENU EN TOURNANT EN DEDANS—COUNT *three:* Draw the left pointe into fifth position front and rise onto the right pointe, turning en dedans (to right) to face the back, bringing the left foot front fifth position sur les pointes. With a demi-détourné, pivot a half-turn to the right to face front. Change feet on the pivot so that the right foot is front in fifth position sur les pointes. Arms move through preparatory position into first position en avant. Head follows movement of the body (do not spot).

DÉGAGÉ FRONT—COUNT *and:* Demi-plié on the left foot and dégagé the right foot front effacé in preparation for arabesque to corner 2. Arms are in first position en avant. Look to corner 2.

PIQUÉ ARABESQUE—COUNT *four:* Piqué onto the right pointe toward corner 2 and raise the left foot back in first arabesque; immediately fondu on the right foot with the left leg dégagé back. Arms move to first arabesque position, raising scarf front with a sweeping movement of the right arm. Look toward the scarf.

TEN

This combination remains in place and then turns toward corner 6.

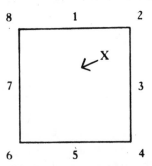

BALLOTTÉ EN AVANT—COUNT *one:* Spring off the right foot and, bending the left leg, spring into the air bending both knees and drawing the feet toward each other. Come down on the left foot in demi-plié, at the same time opening the right leg with a small développé to pointe tendue front in effacé. The body leans slightly back. Look to left toward the arms. Both arms extend toward the left, parallel to each other, with a sweeping movement of the scarf.

HOLD POSE—COUNT *and, two:* Hold pose as above, pointe tendue front in effacé.

BALLOTTÉ EN ARRIÈRE—COUNT *three:* Spring off the left foot and, bending the right leg, spring into the air bending both knees and drawing the feet toward each other. Come down on the right foot in demi-plié, at the same time opening the left leg with a small développé to pointe tendue back in effacé. Body leans slightly forward. Look to right toward the arms. Both arms move downward parallel to each other and extend forward toward the right with a sweeping movement of the scarf.

HOLD POSE—COUNT *and, four:* Hold pose as above, pointe tendue back in effacé.

Ballotté en arrière

Dégagé right foot—count *and:*   With a slight turn to the left, face back toward corner 6 and step on the left foot front with demi-plié. Dégagé right leg to second position a few inches off the floor, at the same time changing position of the body to face corner 4. The left arm opens strongly to second position so that both arms are in second position. Look over the right shoulder toward corner 6 to fix the spot for the following turn.

Single or double piqué tour en dehors—count *five:*   Draw the right foot sur la pointe in front of the left foot, at the same time raising the left foot to retiré in front of the right knee. Execute a single or double turn en dehors to the left on the right pointe. Arms close to first position en avant. Head spots to corner 6.

Fourth position plié à quart effacé—count *six:*   After single turn (which is really only a half-turn) or double turn (which is really only a turn and a half), change spot to front corner 2. Close into fourth position plié à quart effacé with right leg in demi-plié in front. Extend left leg back with knee straight; foot flat on the floor. With a sweeping movement of the scarf, both arms extend toward the right parallel to each other with the right arm higher. Look toward corner 2.

Hold pose—count *and, seven:*   Hold pose as above in fourth position plié à quart effacé.

ELEVEN

This combination moves in a circular manner away from the audience and then returns to corner 2.

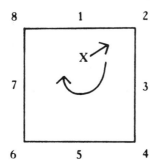

This combination is similar to combination NINE.

PIQUÉ INTO FOURTH ARABESQUE—COUNT *one:* Demi-plié on the right foot and, with a dégagé forward with left foot, piqué on left pointe to corner 2 and raise the right leg back in fourth arabesque croisé. Arms move into fourth arabesque position with the left arm front; the scarf is held in the right hand, which is back. Look front over the left shoulder épaulé.

GLISSADE BACK WITH A HALF-TURN—COUNT *two:* Same as combination NINE—count *one.*

SAUTÉ À LA SECONDE EN TOURNANT—COUNT *three:* Same as combination NINE—count *two.*

ASSEMBLÉ SOUTENU EN TOURNANT EN DEDANS SUR LES POINTES—COUNT *and:* Same as combination NINE—count *three.*

DEMI-PLIÉ FIFTH POSITION CROISÉ—COUNT *four:* The right foot is front in fifth position sur les pointes, demi-plié in fifth position very quickly. The right arm is in first position en avant; the left arm is in second. Look toward the audience.

TWELVE

This combination moves toward side 3 and then toward corner 2.

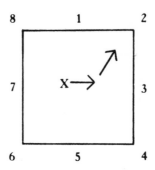

EMBOÎTÉ EN TOURNANT SUR LES POINTES—COUNT *one, and two:* Same as combination TWO—count *one, and two.*

ASSEMBLÉ SOUTENU EN TOURNANT EN DEDANS—COUNT *three:* Piqué toward corner 2 on the right pointe, drawing left foot to front of the right foot in fifth position sur les pointes. Then turn the body to the right with a pivot on both feet with a half-turn to the right. Demi-détourné to right changing feet to finish with the right foot fifth position front sur les pointes. The right arm opens and then closes to meet left arm in first position front en avant on the turn.

FOURTH POSITION PLIÉ À QUART—COUNT *and, four:* Right foot opens with weight forward to fourth position, effacé to corner 2 (the right foot is in demi-plié). Left foot is extended back with foot flat on the floor in preparation for the following pirouette. (Do not put too much weight forward.) The right arm is in first position en avant; left arm opens to second position. Look toward corner 2.

DOUBLE PIROUETTE EN DEDANS—COUNT *and, five:* Dégagé the left leg to a low second position en l'air ($45°$). With a relevé on the right pointe, bring left foot to the front of the right knee and turn to the right executing a double pirouette. Both arms open to second position on dégagé and close to meet each other in first position en avant during the turn. The head spots to corner 2.

Fondu into third arabesque

FONDU INTO THIRD ARABESQUE—COUNT *and, six:*   Finish pirouette by closing into third arabesque croisée fondue, with the left leg front demi-plié toward corner 2. The right leg is extended back in third arabesque croisé. The right arm opens to the front with a flourish of the scarf as left arm opens to second position. Look toward scarf.

Notes

1.   Instead of the entrechat-six de volée (as in combination FIVE—count *and, four*) the following alternative can be substituted:

ASSEMBLÉ BATTU PORTÉ—COUNT *and, four:*   Brush right leg to a low second position, at the same time traveling to the right toward side 3. Bring the left foot in front of the right foot en l'air, beating the calves of the legs together with the left foot in front. Change feet just before alighting in fifth position demi-plié, so that the right foot is in front croisé. Arms open to second position allongé with the right arm higher than the left arm. The right arm flicks the scarf with a movement of the elbow and wrist. Look toward the scarf.

RAYMONDA'S
SCARF VARIATION

From the Ballet

Raymonda

Leningrad Kirov Version

Cynthia Gregory

dances Raymonda's Scarf Variation in RAYMONDA.

———————————————————————

RAYMONDA'S
SCARF VARIATION
Leningrad Kirov Version

Prima ballerina variation from Act I of the ballet *Raymonda*. Music by Alexander Glazunov. Choreography after Marius Petipa. As revived by Konstantin Sergeyev in 1948. Notated by Laurencia Klaja. Tempo 2/4, allegretto.

Recommended Recording

Raymonda Suite by Alexander Glazunov. Conducted by Yevgeny Svetlanov, with the Bolshoi Theatre Orchestra. Angel Melodiya SR-40172, side 1, Act I.

This variation is called "Prelude and Variation" and follows immediately after "Prelude and Romanesca." ("Raymonda's Scarf Variation" is sung by the voice of the solo harp.

Piano Music

Raymonda, Ballet in three acts by Alexander Glazunov. Edition of
M. P. Belaieff. CAT. NO. BEL-317. Sole agents: C. F. Peters Corp., 373
Park Avenue, New York, N.Y. 10016. Act I, page 38, "Prélude et
Variation."

Follows immediately after "Prélude et Romanesca." "Raymonda
passe son luth à une de ses compagnes et vient montrer une variante"
are the stage directions written on the piano score.

Comments

As a contrast to the variation as taught by Madame Shollar, I have
included this version of Raymonda's Scarf variation, which is taken
from a later version of *Raymonda,* as revised by Konstantin Sergeyev
for the Leningrad Kirov Ballet. There is a similarity to the earlier version in the opening demi-fouetté and later in the arabesque voyagée,
but otherwise this variation is totally different. In my opinion, the un-
surpassable Raymonda is the one danced by Irina Kolpakova (accent
on the third syllable) of the Leningrad Kirov Ballet, in a role that she
seemed born to dance. With the utmost ease, grace, and stamina she
accomplished the most difficult technical feats in this long and taxing
role, with its many entrances, codas, variations, and pas de deux.

In this version, the mood of Raymonda during this variation is
similar to that of Prince Siegfried in the first act of *Swan Lake.* She
has come of age to marry and, leaving the days of her youth behind
her, she must choose a husband who she hopes will fulfill her roman-
tic dreams of love. Therefore there is a slight tinge of sadness to her
gay mood as she visits with her friends at the end of her birthday celebration. She sits in front of the tapestry that she has received, among
other gifts, and upon which appears a portrait of the knight, Jean de
Brienne, who has asked for her hand in marriage, but whom she has
never met. With a long scarf draped about her shoulders she plays a

small, harplike instrument while her two friends dance with their cavaliers. She then hands the instrument to one of her friends and, taking the scarf from her shoulders, she moves to the center of the room and prepares to dance the variation, after which, bidding her friends goodbye and sitting down again in the chair, she will fall asleep and dream that Jean de Brienne steps out of the tapestry and dances with her.

The work with the scarf is more difficult in this version because instead of just being held in the right hand throughout, as in Madame Shollar's version, the scarf here is sometimes held in both hands and is also changed from one hand to the other, according to the demands of the choreography.

INTRODUCTION

Move in a semi-circle from side 7 toward side 3 turning around to the right, toward corner 6, and ending at center stage.

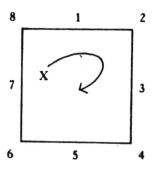

COUNT *one* THROUGH *eight:* With the long scarf held with both hands slightly to the left in front of the body, slowly walk sur les demi-pointes around to center stage. Pointe tendue right foot front croisé with bent knee, tip of right toe resting on the floor.

COUNT *nine* THROUGH *twelve:* Stand with the body inclined slightly to the right. Look down at the scarf, which is now held slightly to the right.

ONE

This combination moves to the right toward side 3.

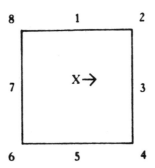

RELEVÉ-DÉVELOPPÉ EN FACE—COUNT *one:* Step forward toward audience onto the right foot in demi-plié, bringing the left foot sur le cou-de-pied back, and continue with a relevé on the right leg with a développé à la seconde with the left leg (90°). Both arms move upward with the scarf so that it is held over the head with the arms extended. Body faces front en face; look toward the audience.

DEMI-FOUETTÉ EN DEHORS INTO ARABESQUE EFFACÉE FONDUE—COUNT *two:* Continue the movement so that the left leg rotates on the pivot of the hip into arabesque effacée, at the same time turning the body to face side 3 and coming down in demi-plié on the right leg. With the scarf still held in both hands, move both arms to extend front with the right arm higher than the left arm. Head turns to the left; look toward the audience.

TOMBÉ BACK—COUNT *three:* Fall back onto left leg in demi-plié, at the same time raising the right leg dégagé front facing side 3. Scarf is held in both hands in front of the body, which faces side 3.

PɪQUÉ ɪɴᴛᴏ ᴀᴛᴛɪᴛᴜᴅᴇ ʙᴀᴄᴋ—ᴄᴏᴜɴᴛ *and, four:* Step forward onto
the right foot in demi-plié, bringing the left foot dégagé front,
and piqué forward onto the left pointe toward side 3, at the same
time raising the right leg back in attitude. Raise the scarf above
the head with both hands, stretching the arms and body slightly
back with shoulders turned slightly toward the audience. Head
inclines to the left.

TWO

*This combination moves diagonally back toward corner 4 and then
moves left toward side 7 to center stage.*

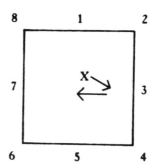

PɪQUÉ ʙᴀᴄᴋ ᴡɪᴛʜ ᴘᴇᴛɪᴛ ʙᴀᴛᴛᴇᴍᴇɴᴛ ʙᴀᴛᴛᴜ sᴜʀ ʟᴇ ᴄᴏᴜ-ᴅᴇ-ᴘɪᴇᴅ
ꜰʀᴏɴᴛ—ᴄᴏᴜɴᴛ *one:* Releasing scarf from the right hand and
with a demi-plié on the left foot, piqué back onto the right pointe
toward corner 4, at the same time bringing the left foot sur le
cou-de-pied front. Scarf, which is now held in the left hand, is
brought across front of body while the head looks right toward
corner 4. The right arm is in second position. Body faces corner
2, with the shoulders écarté to corner 8.

OPEN LEG ÉCARTÉ (45°) AND TOMBÉ FORWARD—COUNT *and, two:* Remaining sur la pointe on the right foot, open the left foot toward corner 8 at 45°, at the same time flourishing the scarf toward corner 8. Body and head are écarté to corner 8. The right arm, which is in second position, rises slightly as the left arm opens outward to flourish the scarf.

—Tombé forward into demi-plié on the left foot, at the same time bringing the right foot sur le cou-de-pied back croisé. Scarf, head, and body remain the same.

PIQUÉ BACK WITH PETIT BATTEMENT BATTU SUR LE COU-DE-PIED FRONT—COUNT *three:* Same as count *one.*

OPEN LEG ÉCARTÉ (45°) AND TOMBÉ FORWARD—COUNT *and, four:* Same as count *and, two.*

PAS DE BOURRÉE COURU EN CINQUIÈME LEFT TOWARD SIDE 7 STOPPING AT CENTER STAGE—COUNT *and, five, six, and, seven:* Both arms are in front of the body in low first position as the right hand again takes the end of the scarf so that it is held by both hands. The body and head incline forward facing side 3.

—Step under onto the right pointe and bourrée with ten tiny steps in fifth position sur les pointes to the left to stage center. The arms, holding the scarf, gradually rise upward over the head in a semi-circle moving from the right upward with elbows straight. Body first inclines to the right and then gradually straightens so that body and head face audience.

THREE

Repeat combination ONE exactly.

FOUR

This combination moves diagonally back toward corner 4 and then moves left to center stage.

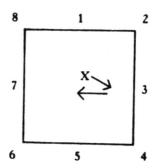

Repeat combination TWO—count *one* through *four* exactly. Continue as follows.

PAS DE BOURRÉE COURU EN CINQUIÈME LEFT TOWARD SIDE 7—COUNT *and, five, six:* Same as combination TWO—count *and, five, six,* but instead of ten tiny steps, there will be only six. Change scarf so that it is held forward in the right hand only, with the left arm in second position.

GLISSADE (NO CHANGE)—COUNT *and, seven:* Tombé-coupé forward in demi-plié onto the right foot, with a dégagé to the side of the left foot, and execute a glissade to the left toward side 7 without changing the feet. Body faces audience. Look left toward corner 8. Scarf remains held in the right hand in second position.

FIVE

This combination moves left toward side 7 and then right toward side 3.

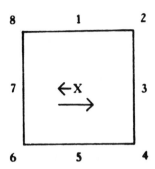

PIQUÉ TO SIDE WITH RETIRÉ—COUNT *one:* Dégagé left foot to side 7 and piqué onto left pointe, at the same time bringing the right foot retiré to front of left knee. The right hand with scarf moves upward in second position with a flourish of the scarf. The left arm is in second position. Body faces audience, look toward the scarf.

PIQUÉ TO SIDE WITH ATTITUDE BACK CROISÉ—COUNT *two:* Tombé forward onto the right foot demi-plié with the left leg dégagé back effacé and immediately piqué onto the left pointe to the side toward side 7. At the same time bring the right foot to attitude back croisé. The right hand, still holding the scarf, moves forward across the body with a circular movement upward and outward flourishing the scarf to the right. Body inclines to the left; look to the right and upward toward the scarf.

STEP ON RIGHT FOOT, STEP ON LEFT FOOT—COUNT *three:* Demi-plié on the left foot and step forward onto the right leg in demi-plié toward side 3. Step forward onto the left foot in demi-plié in preparation for the following grand jeté. Arms are in second position with the scarf in the right hand. Body and head face side 3.

GRAND JETÉ EN AVANT—COUNT *and, four:* Throw the right leg forward in grand battement and jump into the air toward side 3 with the left leg dégagé back effacé, coming down on the right foot in demi-plié with the left leg dégagé back in arabesque effacée. The right hand moves inward and then outward with a flourish of the scarf. The left arm remains in second position. The body and head face side 3.

SIX

This combination moves in place en tournant and then moves backward toward center stage.

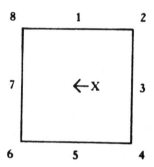

THREE HOPS ON FLAT FOOT SUR PLACE EN TOURNANT EN DEDANS IN ARABESQUE—COUNT *five, and six:* Hop on the right foot flat in demi-plié in place with the left leg in arabesque while turning a third of a turn to the right on each hop so as to again finish facing side 3. Scarf remains held in the right hand with the right arm front in first arabesque position. The left arm is in second position. Look over the right arm.

FOUR HOPS ON FLAT FOOT IN ARABESQUE VOYAGÉE BACK—COUNT *and seven, and eight:* Hop on the right foot flat in demi-plié with the left leg in arabesque effacée while moving backward toward side 7. The scarf held in the right hand is first flourished downward and then upward. Body faces side 3; look toward the scarf.

SEVEN

Repeat combination FIVE exactly.

EIGHT

Repeat combination SIX exactly.

NINE

This combination remains in place at center stage.

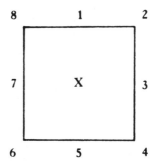

POINTE TENDUE EFFACÉE FRONT—COUNT *one:* Bring the left foot
through retiré and pointe tendue left foot effacé front, at the
same time turning the body to face corner 8 with the right leg in
demi-plié. The scarf is in the right hand and the left arm is in
second position. Raise the right arm upward and inward with a
circular motion and then downward toward the left foot. Body
inclines forward; look toward left pointe.

RELEVÉ INTO ATTITUDE CROISÉ BACK—COUNT *two:* Passing the left
foot through first position demi-plié, relevé onto the right pointe
and raise the left leg back into attitude croisée. The right hand is
holding scarf as the right arm moves upward and outward in a
circular motion over the head with a flourish. Body faces corner 8
and inclines to the right. Head follows movement of the scarf.

SLOW PAS DE BOURRÉE PIQUÉ CHANGÉE SUR LES POINTES SUR
PLACE—COUNT *three, and four:* Remaining sur la pointe with
straight knee on the right leg, bring the left foot back to fifth position, stepping on the left pointe, and bring the right foot sur le
cou-de-pied front.

—Step the right foot to second position on the floor sur les
pointes.

—Remaining sur la pointe with straight knee on the right leg,
bring the left foot sur le cou-de-pied front. The left hand takes
the end of the scarf as the scarf is raised and extended over the
head with both hands. Head and body incline to the left as the
left shoulder comes forward.

TEN

This combination remains sur place and then moves toward side 3.

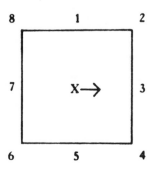

FAST PAS DE BOURRÉE PIQUÉ CHANGÉE SUR LES POINTES SUR
PLACE—COUNT *one, and two:* Same as combination NINE—
count *three, and four,* but done to the opposite side at a faster
tempo. The arms remain extended above the head holding the
scarf.

FAST PAS DE BOURRÉE PIQUÉ CHANGÉE SUR LES POINTES SUR
PLACE—COUNT *three, and four:* Same as combination NINE—
count *three, and four,* but done at a faster tempo. The arms
remain extended above the head holding the scarf.

PAS DE BOURRÉE COURU EN PREMIÈRE BACKWARD—COUNT *and, five,
six, and, seven:* Tombé forward onto the left foot demi-plié,
bringing the right foot sur le cou-de-pied back effacé. The right
hand releases the scarf as the left arm with the scarf opens outward and downward. Body and head incline forward facing
corner 8.

—Step back onto the right pointe and bourrée sur les pointes
backward toward side 3 in first position with four tiny steps. The
left arm flourishes the scarf toward the left upward and downward twice. Body straightens and faces corner 8; look at scarf.
(Do not travel too much.)

ELEVEN

Repeat combination NINE to the opposite side.

TWELVE

This combination remains sur place and then moves toward side 3.

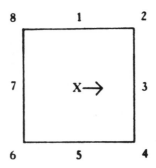

Repeat combination TEN count *one* through *four,* to the opposite side. Continue as follows.

TWO CHAÎNÉS-DÉBOULÉS—COUNT *and, five:* Step forward onto the right foot in demi-plié toward side 3. Execute two chaîné-déboulé turns holding the scarf in front of body with the arms in low first position. Head spots to side 3.

FINAL POSE—COUNT *and, six* (HOLD): Step forward onto the right foot in demi-plié and immediately straighten the knee. At the same time bring the left foot effacé back pointe tendue with knee relaxed so that both knees are together. Raise scarf in front of body with both hands and bring it over the head so that scarf is placed around the shoulders with both arms crossed in front of the body. Head and body face side 3 with head inclined slightly back.

PRINCESS AURORA'S
ACT I VARIATION

From the Ballet

The Sleeping Beauty

La Belle au Bois Dormant

Ludmilla Semenyaka

as Princess Aurora in THE SLEEPING BEAUTY.

Natalia Makarova

as Princess Aurora in THE SLEEPING BEAUTY.

———————————

Margot Fonteyn

as Princess Aurora in THE SLEEPING BEAUTY.

PRINCESS AURORA'S
ACT I VARIATION

Prima ballerina variation for Princess Aurora from Act I of *The Sleeping Beauty* ballet. Music by Peter Ilyich Tchaikovsky. Choreography after Marius Petipa. An adaptation of the variation as taught in the classes of Ludmilla Shollar, Anatole Vilzak, and Barbara Fallis. Adapted and notated by Laurencia Klaja. Tempo 3/8, allegro moderato.

Recommended Recordings

1. *Tchaikovsky Greatest Ballets, Vol. 3, Suite from The Sleeping Beauty*. Conducted by Eugene Ormandy, with the Philadelphia Orchestra. RCA Red Seal, ARL 1-0169 STEREO, side B: Act I. Pas d'action.

"Aurora's Variation" follows immediately after the "Dance of the Maids of Honor." For the final circle, the music should be cut after the first sixteen counts.

2. *The Sleeping Beauty Ballet, Complete*. Richard Bonynge, conductor, with the National Philharmonic Orchestra. London Records,

London FFRR, CSA 2316, side 3: Act I. "Variation d'Aurore" follows "Danse des demoiselles d'honneur et des pages." In this recording an additional cut of sixteen counts should be made in the repeat which follows combination THIRTEEN just before the turns in a circle. This can be accomplished by making a tape of the variation and pressing the "pause" key of the tape recorder just before the music is repeated. Then after the sixteen counts have played on the record, press the "play" key again to resume the recording of the rest of the variation on the tape.

Piano Music

Complete Piano Music for The Sleeping Beauty Ballet, by Peter Ilyich Tchaikovsky. Act I, No. 8, Pas d'action, Aurora's Variation, on page 79. The sixteen bars of music should be cut right after combination THIRTEEN, where the music is repeated, and at the end of the sixteen-count circle of twelve piqué turns and two chaîné-déboulé turns that ends in either fifth position sur les pointes or fourth position plié à quart. Published by The Tschaikovsky Foundation, 1950.

Comments

La Belle au Bois Dormant and *Spiashchaya Krasavitsa* are the French and Russian titles of what is known in English as *The Sleeping Beauty* ballet, which was first given in St. Petersburg in 1890. At its premiere the Italian ballerina Carlotta Brianza danced Princess Aurora and Pavel Gerdt, Prince Désiré. In those days, Italian ballerinas were brought into Russia to dance leading roles because the Russian ballerinas had not yet developed the brilliant technique taught by the Italian ballet masters.

This variation from Act I for Princess Aurora follows shortly after the "Rose Adagio," famous for its long-held balances en pointe in attitude effacée for the ballerina. In the early ballets such as *Giselle* and *Coppélia,* a pantomime scene called a pas d'action was inserted between the dances in order to tell the story of the ballet. Later at the Russian Imperial Theatre a pas d'action was a dance scene in a story ballet used to develop the plot. This variation is part of such a pas d'action, which consists of: Adagio, Dance of the Maids of Honor and the Pages, Aurora's Variation, and Coda.

The court of King Florestan XXIV is celebrating the sixteenth birthday of his daughter, Princess Aurora, who has just become of marriageable age and is expected to choose a husband from one of her four cavaliers, each of whom presents her with a rose.

The *Borzoi Book of Ballets* gives a description of the ballet *Princess Aurora,* a one-act version of *The Sleeping Beauty:*

"Aurora's variation concludes the series. Difficult and ungracious, it may acquire a certain grandeur from a fine performance. Aurora runs on, as though greeting the guests, bowing slightly to the King and Queen. She does a glissade, arabesque, and, using a transitional step (failli), poses en attitude, arms in fifth position en haut, followed by a fourth position with expanding port-de-bras; again glissade, arabesque, bourrée moving diagonally, rond de jambe, retiré; hops en attitude en avant. She retraces her diagonal with fifth position emboîtés, does a preparation leading to a pirouette ending with a large fourth position. The next sequence begins with glissade, arabesque, and continues with a circle of piqué turns covering the entire stage. The variation ends with chaînés and a pas de chat into a fourth position, with arms outstretched. Any charm this variation may have comes entirely from the ballerina's ability to phrase her steps musically."*

INTRODUCTION

Stand center stage with the right foot pointe tendue back croisé, knee relaxed. Arms are in low second position at the sides of the tutu, with elbows slightly rounded. Look toward the audience. Wait for the repeated theme of two notes that comes toward the end of the introduction to the variation to begin the following counts.

Count *and, one* through *and, eight:* Wait in the same pose as described above.

* *Grace Robert,* Borzoi Book of Ballets (*New York: Alfred A. Knopf, 1946*). *Now out of print.*

Count *and, nine:* Demi-plié on the left foot, at the same time transferring the weight back onto the right foot in demi-plié and immediately straightening the right knee. Pointe tendue left foot front croisé with knee straight. Arms remain in low second; look right toward corner 2.

Count *and, ten:* Bring right hand to breast and extend it to the right while looking right toward side 3 as if asking permission of the court on this side to dance for them.

Count *and, eleven:* The right hand remains extended toward the right corner while the left hand moves to the breast and extends to the left while looking left toward side 7 as if asking permission of the court on this side to dance for them also.

Count *and, twelve:* Stand and wait with the left foot pointe tendue croisée front with knee straight. Both arms are extended forward in a wide first position. Look right again toward corner 2.

ONE

This combination moves toward side 3 and then toward corner 2.

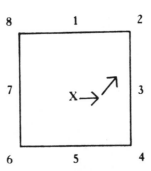

Glissade to right—count *and:* Transfer weight front to the left foot demi-plié; right foot moves to second position with a glissade to the right (side 3), closing the left foot fifth position front demi-plié croisé. Arms are in preparatory position en bas, opening slightly and then closing again. Body is inclined slightly to the right; look to the right.

Piqué arabesque

Piqué arabesque—count *one* (sustained): Demi-plié on the left foot; at the same time dégagé right foot front, turning the body slightly to the right to face side 3. Piqué on right pointe to side 3, raising the left foot back in first arabesque, holding the balance as long as possible. Arms move through first position en avant into first arabesque position, with right arm front. Look toward the right wrist.

Fourth position plié à quart—count *and, two:* Tombé (fall) forward onto the left foot in demi-plié in fourth position croisé front. The right leg is extended back with knee straight and foot flat on the floor, body facing corner 2. Arms are in low second position.† Body inclines slightly to the left; look front.

Glissade to right—count *and:* Dégagé the right foot to second position and glissade to the right to corner 2, changing direction of the body to face corner 8. Close left foot fifth position front demi-plié effacé. Arms are in preparatory position en bas, opening slightly and then closing again. Body and head are facing corner 8.

† *See Note 1, following this variation.*

PIQUÉ ATTITUDE BACK CROISÉ—COUNT *three* (SUSTAINED): Remain in demi-plié on the left foot and dégagé the right foot to second position a few inches above the floor. Piqué on the right pointe slightly forward to corner 8 and raise the left leg back in attitude croisé. Arms pass through first position en avant and raise en haut to third position rounded. Body and head incline slightly backward.

FOURTH POSITION PLIÉ À QUART WITH PORT-DE-BRAS—COUNT *and, four:* Left leg closes back into fourth position plié à quart croisé, with knee straight and foot flat on the floor, right leg in demi-plié front. Arms open outward to second position and pass downward slightly behind the body at hip level. The palms of the hands first open outward away from the body. When the arms reach hip level, the palms are slightly raised and facing backward; then lower and turn the palms to face forward. The body is slightly inclined back while facing corner 8. Head is slightly inclined back and turned to face front. Look downward.

Piqué attitude back croisé

TWO

This combination moves toward side 7 and then toward corner 8.

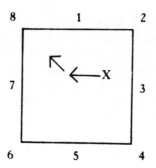

Repeat combination ONE to the opposite side.

GLISSADE TO LEFT; PIQUÉ ARABESQUE—COUNT *and, five* (SUS-
TAINED): Same as combination ONE—count *and, one,* but
done to the opposite side.

FOURTH POSITION PLIÉ À QUART—COUNT *and, six:* Same as combination ONE, count *and, two,* but done to the opposite side.

GLISSADE TO LEFT; PIQUÉ ATTITUDE BACK CROISÉ—COUNT *and,
seven* (SUSTAINED): Same as combination ONE—count *and,
three,* but done to the opposite side.

FOURTH POSITION PLIÉ À QUART WITH PORT-DE-BRAS—COUNT *and,
eight:* Same as combination ONE—count *and, four,* but done
to the opposite side.

THREE

Repeat combination ONE exactly.

FOUR

This combination moves toward side 7 and then to corner 6.

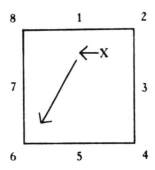

Repeat combination TWO—count *and, five.* Continue as follows.

TOMBÉ-COUPÉ FRONT WITH RIGHT FOOT—COUNT *and:* Fall forward onto the right foot front cutting over left foot, which then rises sur le cou-de-pied back, at center stage. The right arm moves to first position en avant while left arm moves to second position. Body inclines slightly to the right. Look downward over the right shoulder and arm.

PAS DE BOURRÉE COURU BACKWARD IN FIFTH POSITION SUR LES POINTES—COUNT *six, and seven, and:* Piqué on the left foot back sur la pointe. Draw right foot to the left foot in fifth position sur les pointes, and execute eight fast, tiny steps traveling back along the diagonal to corner 6 while facing front. The left arm remains in second position as right arm opens front with elbow extended and gradually moves upward allongé in second position above shoulder level. Shoulders are écarté with right shoulder front to corner 2. Body first inclines slightly forward and then gradually straightens. Look toward the right arm.

FIFTH POSITION SUR LES POINTES—COUNT *eight:* Stop at corner 6 remaining sur les pointes in fifth position with the right foot front croisé. The right arm moves to first position en avant and the left arm remains in second position. Body and head face front.

FIVE‡

This combination moves diagonally forward halfway to corner 2.

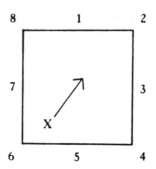

Do not travel too much; by count *eight* you should have reached the halfway point of the diagonal. (Rond de jambe sauté sur la pointe may be substituted for ballonné.)

BALLONNÉ SAUTÉ SUR LA POINTE—COUNT *and:* Remaining sur la pointe on the left foot, bend the left knee and raise the right leg straight to second position in the air ($45°$). Hop slightly sideways toward corner 2, and bring the right foot to the front of left knee in retiré. The left knee remains bent sur la pointe. The right arm moves gracefully in toward the body with the elbow bent and the palm relaxed and facing the body. Left arm is in second position. Look over the right shoulder toward the right arm. Body faces écarté, right shoulder toward corner 2.

PIQUÉ-RETIRÉ SUR LA POINTE—COUNT *one:* Remaining sur la pointe with bent knee on the left leg, piqué on the right pointe sideways to corner 2, at the same time raising the left foot retiré back of the right knee. The right arm moves gracefully outward and forward to a wide first position on the piqué. The eyes follow the movement of the hand, which opens toward the audience with the palm facing up; the left arm is in second position. On the retiré, the head turns to the left. Look over the left shoulder at the left arm, which moves to first position en avant. Body remains the same.

‡ *See Note 2, following this variation.*

Ballonné sauté sur la pointe; piqué-retiré sur la pointe—
count *and, two:* Same as count *and, one.*

Ballonné sauté sur la pointe; piqué-retiré sur la pointe—
count *and, three:* Same as count *and, one.*

Ballonné sauté sur la pointe; piqué-retiré sur la pointe—
count *and, four:* Same as count *and, one.*

Ballonné sauté sur la pointe; piqué-retiré sur la pointe—
count *and, five:* Same as count *and, one.*

Ballonné sauté sur la pointe; piqué-retiré sur la pointe—
count *and, six:* Same as count *and, one.*

Ballonné sauté sur la pointe; piqué-retiré sur la pointe—
count *and, seven:* Same as count *and, one.*

Ballonné sauté sur la pointe; piqué-retiré sur la pointe—
count *and, eight:* Same as count *and, one.*

SIX

This combination continues the diagonal to corner 2.

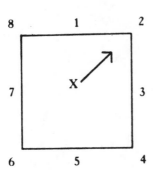

Ballonné sauté sur la pointe; piqué-retiré sur la pointe—
count *and, one:* Same as combination FIVE—count *and, one.*

BALLONNÉ SAUTÉ SUR LA POINTE; PIQUÉ-RETIRÉ SUR LA POINTE—
COUNT *and, two:* Same as combination FIVE—count *and, one.*

BALLONNÉ SAUTÉ SUR LA POINTE; PIQUÉ-RETIRÉ SUR LA POINTE—
COUNT *and, three:* Same as combination FIVE—count *and, one.*

BALLONNÉ SAUTÉ SUR LA POINTE; PIQUÉ-RETIRÉ SUR LA POINTE—
COUNT *and, four:* Same as combination FIVE—count *and, one.*

BALLONNÉ SAUTÉ SUR LA POINTE; PIQUÉ-RETIRÉ SUR LA POINTE—
COUNT *and, five:* Same as combination FIVE—count *and, one.*

BALLONNÉ SAUTÉ SUR LA POINTE; PIQUÉ-RETIRÉ SUR LA POINTE—
COUNT *and, six:* Same as combination FIVE—count *and, one.*

Fourth position plié à quart

BOURRÉE CHANGÉE SUR PLACE—COUNT *and seven, and:* Remaining sur la pointe on the right foot, return left foot to fifth position back sur les pointes and execute three tiny steps in place very quickly, like a trill.*

—Remaining sur les pointes, move left foot to fifth position front, opening just enough to pass the heel of the right foot, as the right foot changes to fifth position back.

—Remaining sur les pointes, move the right foot to fifth position front, opening just enough to pass the heel of the left foot, as the left foot changes to fifth position back.

—Remaining sur les pointes, move the left foot to fifth position front, opening just enough to pass the heel of the right foot, as the right foot changes to fifth position back. Arms are in low second position. Body inclines slightly forward; look downward.

FOURTH POSITION PLIÉ À QUART—COUNT *eight:*† Open the right foot to fourth position croisé back and demi-plié on the left foot, which is front, while the right foot, with the knee straight, is extended back with foot flat on the floor. Arms open to a wide first position en avant. Body inclines slightly to the left. Look over the left shoulder toward the audience.

SEVEN

This combination retraces the diagonal toward corner 6.

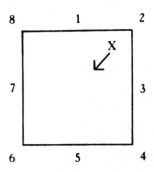

EMBOÎTÉ FRONT SAUTÉ WITH RIGHT LEG—COUNT *one:* Spring up

---

* *See Note 3, following this variation.*
† *For an alternate version, see Note 4, following this variation.*

slightly off left foot and bring right foot front à terre with straight knee, coming down on the left foot in demi-plié with right leg remaining front. (Keep the heel well forward on the floor.) Arms begin to move to first position en avant. Body inclines forward from the waist. Look toward the arms.

EMBOÎTÉ FRONT SAUTÉ WITH LEFT LEG—COUNT *two:* Spring up slightly off right foot and bring left foot front à terre with straight knee, coming down on the right foot in demi-plié with left leg remaining front. Arms are in first position en avant. Body begins to straighten as head follows movement of the arms.

EMBOÎTÉ FRONT SAUTÉ WITH RIGHT LEG—COUNT *three:* Same as count *one,* except that the arms are changing. Arms begin to rise to third position en haut rounded. Body continues to straighten. Look toward the arms.

EMBOÎTÉ FRONT SAUTÉ WITH LEFT LEG—COUNT *four:* Same as count *two,* except that the arms are changing. Arms continue to rise to third position en haut rounded as body continues to straighten and head follows movement of the arms.

EMBOÎTÉ FRONT SAUTÉ WITH RIGHT LEG—COUNT *five:*‡ Same as count *one,* except that the arms are changing. Arms are in third position en haut rounded. Body has straightened. Look upward toward the arms.

EMBOÎTÉ FRONT SAUTÉ WITH LEFT LEG—COUNT *six:* Same as count *two,* except for the arms. Arms are in third position en haut rounded. Body is straight; look upward toward the arms.

PAS DE BOURRÉE IN FIFTH POSITION SUR PLACE—COUNT *seven:* Bring the left foot in front of the right foot and step on the full pointe, at the same time rising on the right pointe into fifth position sur les pointes with left foot front. Then execute two tiny bourrée steps in place: transfer weight left foot, right foot, left foot, right foot. Arms remain in third position en haut rounded. Look toward corner 2.

FOURTH POSITION DEMI-PLIÉ—COUNT *eight:* Open the right foot to fourth position back croisé and simultaneously demi-plié on both right and left legs equally in preparation for pirouette. Arms open outward to second position. Right arm continues to third

‡ *See Note 5, following this variation.*

arabesque position en avant with palm down, left arm is in second position. Body is straight. Look toward corner 2 as before.

DOUBLE OR TRIPLE PIROUETTE EN DEHORS—Anticipate the music and start the turn ahead of the music. An embellished chord marks the end of the pirouette. With a relevé on the left pointe and raising the right foot to retiré in front of the left knee, execute multiple turns to the right. The right arm executes a slight stroke inward and forward with the palm down, and then moves outward toward second position as the palm turns to face the body, starting the momentum of the turn. Then the left arm gives additional momentum as it swings inward to first position en avant where it meets the right arm moving inward to first position, palms facing the body. Body remains straight as head spots to corner 2. Finish the pirouette in fourth position plié à quart croisé in demi-plié on left leg with right leg extended back with knee straight and foot flat on the floor. The right arm is extended front with elbow straight as the left arm extends to second position. The palms of the hands are facing downward. Body and head face corner 2.

EIGHT

This combination continues on the diagonal toward corner 6.

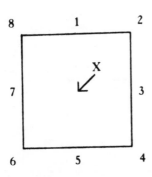

Repeat combination SEVEN, but at the end of the double or triple pirouette the left arm rises to third position rounded as the right arm opens to second position. Body inclines slightly to the right. Look under the arm toward the audience.

NINE

This combination continues on the diagonal to corner 6.

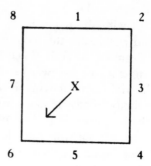

Repeat combination SEVEN, but at the end of the double or triple pirouette both arms rise to third position en haut rounded. Body inclines slightly back with head inclined left and turned toward audience.

TEN

This combination moves right toward side 3 and then
toward corner 2.

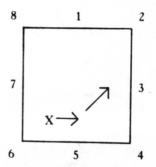

GLISSADE PRESSÉE TO RIGHT—COUNT *one:* Right foot moves in a quick glissade passing through second position à terre to finish in fifth position front croisé demi-plié moving to the right toward corner 2. (This step resembles a small assemblé.) Arms open outward to second position and right arm continues through preparatory position to first position en avant. Left arm remains in second position. Body inclines slightly to the right. Look to the right over the right arm.

GLISSADE PRESSÉE TO RIGHT—COUNT *two:* Right foot executes another quick glissade to the right without changing feet and finishes in fifth position croisé with right foot front demi-plié. The right arm remains in first position and left arm remains in second. Body en face inclines slightly to the right. Look over the right arm.

PAS DE BOURRÉE COURU EN CINQUIÈME TO THE RIGHT—COUNT *three, four, five, six, seven:* Step toward the right (side 3) on the right pointe, drawing the left foot behind the right foot sur les pointes in fifth position. Move toward side 3 with ten tiny steps, while the arms execute the following port-de-bras: The right arm moves gradually en haut to third position rounded, passing through first position en avant, while the left arm remains in second position. Body inclines slightly to the right. Look toward corner 2 and then toward the right wrist.

FOURTH POSITION DEMI-PLIÉ—COUNT *eight:* From fifth position sur les pointes front, the right foot opens back in fourth position croisé, both legs in demi-plié. The right arm moves outward and downward and then extends front in third arabesque position with palm down. The left arm is in second position in preparation for pirouette. Body and head face corner 2.

DOUBLE PIROUETTE EN DEHORS FOLLOWED BY A DÉTOURNÉ. Anticipate the music and start the turn ahead of the music. An embellished chord marks the end of the pirouette and détourné. Pirouette ends with the right foot back in fifth position demi-plié facing corner 2. Then make a quick relevé on both pointes into fifth position with a change of the right foot to fifth position front sur les pointes as the body turns to the right and faces front so that the right foot is front croisé. Hold the right heel strongly. From first position en avant, both arms rise quickly to third position en haut rounded. Body inclines slightly to the right; look toward audience.

ELEVEN

This combination moves from side to side at center stage.

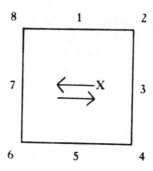

PAS DE BOURRÉE COURU EN CINQUIÈME—COUNT *and, one:* Remaining sur les pointes in fifth position, quickly move left with four tiny steps toward side 7; right foot is front. Arms open gradually outward to second position allongé with the left arm higher, palms downward. Body faces the audience. Look left toward corner 8.

ATTITUDE FRONT SAUTÉ SUR LA POINTE—COUNT *and, two:* Remaining sur la pointe on the left foot, bend the left knee and, raising right leg to attitude front, hop on the left pointe. Arms have reached second position allongé with left arm slightly higher than shoulder level, with elbow extended and palm facing downward. The right arm is slightly lower than shoulder level, in proportion to the left arm. Elbow is extended with palm facing downward. Body inclines slightly to the right. Look left toward the left wrist (or toward one of the four cavaliers).

PAS DE BOURRÉE COURU EN CINQUIÈME—COUNT *and, three:* Remaining sur la pointe on the left foot, lower right leg to fifth position front sur les pointes and continue with four fast, tiny steps to the right. Arms level to second position, and the left arm moves

Attitude front sauté
sur la pointe

gradually inward and downward to first position en avant; the right arm moves gradually upward to third position en haut rounded. Body remains facing the audience. Look right toward corner 2.

ATTITUDE BACK SAUTÉ SUR LA POINTE—COUNT *and, four:* Remaining sur la pointe on the right foot, bend the right knee and, raising the left leg to attitude back croisé, hop on the right pointe. The right arm is in third position en haut and the left arm is in first position en avant. Body inclines slightly to the left. Look under the right arm toward corner 2 (or to one of the four cavaliers).

TWELVE

This combination continues to move from side to side at center stage.

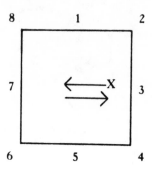

PAS DE BOURRÉE COURU EN CINQUIÈME—COUNT *and, five:* Same as combination ELEVEN—count *and, one,* except that the right arm moves downward and inward to first position en avant to meet the left arm in first position en avant.

ATTITUDE FRONT SAUTÉ SUR LA POINTE—COUNT *and, six:* Same as combination ELEVEN—count *and, two:* Both arms gradually open to second position allongé as before.

PAS DE BOURRÉE COURU EN CINQUIÈME—COUNT *and, seven:* Same as combination ELEVEN—count *and, three.*

ATTITUDE BACK SAUTÉ SUR LA POINTE—COUNT *and, eight:* Same as combination ELEVEN—count *and, four.*

THIRTEEN

Repeat combination ELEVEN exactly.

FOURTEEN

This combination moves from side 3 toward side 7 and then moves to corner 8.

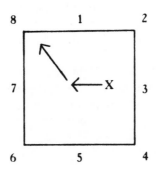

GLISSADE—COUNT *and, five:* Remaining sur la pointe on the right foot, return left foot back sur les pointes fifth position with a passing movement into fifth position demi-plié with right foot front croisé. Then with a dégagé of the left foot to second position à terre and a demi-plié on the right leg, execute a glissade to left (side 7), closing right foot front in fifth position croisé demi-plié. The right arm moves downward and inward to first position en avant to meet the left arm in first position en avant. Arms continue downward to preparatory position en bas and open and close slightly on the glissade. Body inclines slightly to the left; look toward left.

PIQUÉ ARABESQUE—COUNT *and:* Dégagé left foot front to side 7 with demi-plié on the right leg, turning the body slightly to the left to face side 7, and step forward to side 7 onto left pointe, raising right leg back into first arabesque position. Arms move through first position en avant to first arabesque position with left arm front. Body is facing side 7; look toward left wrist.

FOURTH POSITION—COUNT *six:* From arabesque position, right foot moves to fourth position front croisé with demi-plié on right foot and left leg extended back with knee straight and foot flat on the floor. Arms move downward to low second position. Body faces corner 8; look toward audience.

RUN SUR LES DEMI-POINTES—COUNT *and, seven:*   Run sur les demi-pointes to downstage corner 8, stepping forward first on left foot, then right foot. Arms are in demi-seconde position. Body inclines slightly forward; look downward.

POINTE TENDUE RIGHT FOOT CROISÉ FRONT—COUNT *and, eight:*   Step to the left side with a demi-plié on the left foot and with a small développé front with right foot, pointe tendue à terre croisé front as preparation for the following circle of turns.

PORT-DE-BRAS—COUNT *and:*   Right arm moves front to first position en avant as left arm moves to second position; then with the left arm remaining in second position, right arm moves upward to third position and quickly opens outward through second position and returns to first position en avant. Body and head face front to the audience.

FIFTEEN

*This combination moves in a circle from corner 8,
ending at corner 2. (A circle is really a square.)*

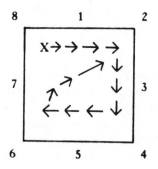

In sixteen counts, make a clockwise circle of twelve piqués tours en dedans ending with chaînés tours and sous-sus sur les pointes. The tempo is fast.

PIQUÉ TOUR EN DEDANS—COUNT *one:* Piqué forward on the right pointe with left foot retiré back of right knee and execute a single piqué turn spotting to side 3. The right arm opens to second position before the turn and on the turn closes to meet the left arm in first position front en avant. Head spots to side 3.

PIQUÉ TOUR EN DEDANS—COUNT *two:* Same as count *one.*

PIQUÉ TOUR EN DEDANS—COUNT *three:* Same as count *one.*

PIQUÉ TOUR EN DEDANS (CHANGE SPOT)—COUNT *four:* Same as count *one,* spotting to side 3, except at the end of the turn the head turns right to look over the right shoulder in order to change the spot to the back on the next turn.

PIQUÉ TOUR EN DEDANS—COUNT *five:* Same as count *one,* except the spot is to the back.

PIQUÉ TOUR EN DEDANS—COUNT *six:* Same as count *one,* except the spot is to the back.

PIQUÉ TOUR EN DEDANS (CHANGE SPOT)—COUNT *seven:* Same as count *one,* except the spot is to the back, and at the end of the turn the head turns to the right, looking over the right shoulder in order to change the spot to side 7 on the following turn.

PIQUÉ TOUR EN DEDANS—COUNT *eight:* Same as count *one,* except the spot is to side 7.

PIQUÉ TOUR EN DEDANS (CHANGE SPOT)—COUNT *one:* Same as count *one,* except the spot is to side 7. At the end of the turn, the head turns to the right to look over the right shoulder in order to change the spot to the front.

PIQUÉ TOUR EN DEDANS (CHANGE SPOT)—COUNT *two:* Same as count *one,* except spot to the front. At the end of the turn, the head turns right to look over the right shoulder in order to change the spot to corner 2.

PIQUÉ TOUR EN DEDANS—COUNT *three:* Same as count *one,* spot to corner 2 on diagonal.

PIQUÉ TOUR EN DEDANS—COUNT *four:* Same as count *one,* except spot to corner 2 on diagonal.

TWO CHAÎNÉS TOURS—COUNT *five, six:* Execute two fast chaîné turns to corner 2. Arms close to first position en avant and remain there. Head spots to corner 2.

SOUS-SUS SUR LES POINTES—COUNT *seven, eight:** At the end of the last chaîné turn, close right foot front in fifth position effacé demi-plié, and sous-sus in place with a relevé in fifth position sur les pointes, changing feet so that the left foot is front croisé. Arms pass through first position en avant and raise en haut to third position rounded on the sous-sus. Body and head face audience.

Notes

1. Margot Fonteyn in the English Royal Ballet production of *The Sleeping Beauty* did this arm movement in a charming way: when she closed into fourth position croisé from arabesque, described in combination ONE—count *and, two,* she brought her left arm front to her breast with the elbow bent and looked to the left at one of her four suitors. This was repeated to the opposite side.

2. Barbara Fallis taught a variant of combination FIVE, that shows greater virtuosity. (It also shortens the length of the diagonal and breaks the monotony of repeating the same steps.)

BALLONNÉ SAUTÉ SUR LA POINTE; PIQUÉ-RETIRÉ SUR LA POINTE—
    COUNT *and, one* THROUGH *and, four:* Same as combination FIVE, count *and, one* through *and, four.*

COUNT *and five, and six, and seven:* Remaining sur la pointe on the left foot, bend left knee and, raising the foot in attitude front, hop on the left pointe three times while turning to the right in place.

COUNT *and, eight:* Return the right front fifth position sur les pointes facing audience. Arms move to third position en haut on this combination. Continue diagonal as outlined in combination SIX.

* *For an alternate version, see Note 6.*

3. TRILL: A vibratory effect. The legs should quiver like the strings of a musical instrument.

4. Instead of fourth position plié à quart, bring the right foot front in fifth position effacé, immediately straightening the knees and inclining the body slightly forward. Look toward the audience.

5. Instead of following the emboîtés with bourrée sur place into fourth position preparation for pirouette, take the preparation for pirouette from a relevé passé with right foot passing from front to fourth position croisé back. Count as follows:

Count *six:* After the fifth emboîté, close the right foot fifth position front demi-plié.

Count *seven:* Relevé passé en arrière.

Count *eight:* Open the right foot to fourth position back croisé.

6. At the end of the last chaîné turn, remaining sur la pointe on the left foot, raise the right foot retiré side of the left knee. Finish in fourth position plié à quart with left leg in demi-plié and right leg extended back straight with foot flat on the floor. Arms are in wide first position front toward the audience.

LILAC FAIRY
VARIATION

From the Ballet

The Sleeping Beauty

La Belle au Bois Dormant

Deanne Bergsma
as the Lilac Fairy in
THE SLEEPING BEAUTY.

Svetlana Beriosova

as the Lilac Fairy in THE SLEEPING BEAUTY.

LILAC FAIRY VARIATION

This is the sixth and last solo variation from the Pas de Six of the six fairies in the Prologue of *The Sleeping Beauty* ballet. MUSIC by Peter Ilyich Tchaikovsky. CHOREOGRAPHY by Feodor Lopukhov, who choreographed it for Lyubov Egorova, who danced it in the Diaghilev production of *The Sleeping Beauty* in London in 1921.* AS TAUGHT by Ludmilla Shollar and Anatole Vilzak. NOTATED by Laurencia Klaja. TEMPO 3/4, tempo di valse.

Recommended Recordings

There are many recordings of the Lilac Fairy variation available in excerpts and complete recordings of *The Sleeping Beauty* ballet.

* *Refer to Mary Clarke and Clement Crisp,* Ballet, An Illustrated History (*New York: Universe Books, 1973*), p. 104.

1. *Excerpts from* The Sleeping Beauty *Ballet,* Boris Khaikin, conductor, with the Orchestra of the Bolshoi Ballet. Westminster Gold Series (Melodiya), wgs-8226, A.B.C. Records, side 1: The Lilac Fairy variation is the sixth of the variations of the fairies from the Pas de Six, immediately preceding the Coda, and may be recognized by its waltz tempo.

2. *The Sleeping Beauty Ballet. Complete.* Richard Bonynge, conductor, with the National Philharmonic Orchestra. London Records, London ffrr, csa 2316. Side 1: Prologue, sixth variation of the Pas de Six, "La Fée des Lilas."

Piano Music

Complete Piano Music for The Sleeping Beauty Ballet, by Peter Ilyich Tchaikovsky. "The Lilac Fairy Variation," p. 31, is the sixth variation of the Pas de Six, in the Prologue. Published by The Tschaikovsky Foundation, 1950.

Comments

In Marius Petipa's first production of *The Sleeping Beauty,* at the Maryinsky Theatre in St. Petersburg, the part of the Lilac Fairy was mimed by Petipa's daughter, Marie, and was a nondancing mimed role, as in the present-day production by Rudolf Nureyev, in which the Principal Fairy dances the variation of the Lilac Fairy in the Prologue. Apparently in those days two people would play the same role in a ballet, one doing the classical dancing, the other, the acting or mime. This might explain why Tchaikovsky wrote a classical variation for the Lilac Fairy.

Why we do not have the original Petipa choreography for the variation may be attributed to the popularity of the Sugar Plum Fairy variation from *The Nutcracker* ballet, which at some point was substituted for the Lilac Fairy variation in the Prologue of *The Sleeping*

Beauty where the six fairies bring gifts to the baby Princess Aurora. Later, because Serge Diaghilev disliked the choreography for Princess Aurora's variation in the last act Pas de Deux, the Sugar Plum Fairy variation was substituted for it in his production. To fill the gap left by the Sugar Plum Fairy's departure from the Prologue, the Lilac Fairy variation was reinstated, with choreography by Feodor Lopukhov, in the style of Petipa.

Lopukhov's choreography for this variation consists of long, sweeping diagonal combinations and is suitable for a soloist of ballerina status with beautiful line, good balance, and strong pirouettes.

To quote again from the *Borzoi Book of Ballets*,† which gives a description of the ballet *Princess Aurora,* a one-act version of *The Sleeping Beauty:*

"The second variation is grave and dignified. In the original production this was the solo of the Lilac Fairy, Aurora's godmother. The entrance from the upstage left is made with a grand rond de jambe en l'air, a fifth position, and a step into arabesque, a large and beautiful movement. The solo ends with a pas de chat and a kneeling pose. It demands from the dancer impeccable line and the ability to sustain its slow rhythm with fluid grace."

INTRODUCTION

Stand at upstage right corner 4.

COUNT *one, two, three:* Stand with right foot point tendue front croisé. Arms are in second position allongé with the left arm higher than the right arm, elbows extended, and palms facing downward. Look toward audience.

† *Grace Robert,* Borzoi Book of Ballets (*New York: Alfred A. Knopf, 1946*). *Now out of print.*

ONE

*This combination moves diagonally downstage
from corner 4 toward corner 8.*

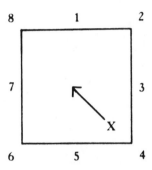

GLISSADE—COUNT *and:* Step forward toward corner 8 on the right foot and glissade (no change) to the left side with right foot closing front in fifth position demi-plié. Arms move downward passing through first position and begin opening into second position. Head inclines to the left.

DEMI-GRAND ROND DE JAMBE EN DEDANS WITH RELEVÉ—COUNT *one:‡* Relevé on the right foot and raise left leg to second position en l'air écarté front. Remaining on pointe on right foot, execute a demi-grand rond de jambe forward to front croisé with left leg. Arms meet in third position en haut in a passing movement as palms turn to face each other and elbows become rounded. Both arms continue moving into allongé position with palms turned outward and downward and elbows extended with the left arm higher than the right arm. Look toward downstage corner 8 and left wrist. Shoulders are écarté front, left shoulder toward corner 8.

DEMI-PLIÉ IN FOURTH POSITION CROISÉ—COUNT *two:* Close left foot fourth position front croisé with demi-plié. Arms move down-

‡ *For a slightly different version, see notes following this variation.*

Demi-grand rond de jambe
en dedans with relevé

---

ward from third position en haut through first position en avant so that the hands are crossed with the left palm a few inches above the right hand and the elbows slightly bent. Head and body incline to the right while facing downstage corner 2.

STEP OVER AND PIQUÉ INTO FIRST ARABESQUE—COUNT *and, three:* From fourth position right foot back, step over with right foot in front of left foot (making sure right toe is pointed) into a demi-plié, raising left foot sur le cou-de-pied back. Arms move to first position en avant. Body straightens and turns to face corner 8. Step onto left pointe and raise right leg back into first arabesque. Arms move to first arabesque position with left arm front. Look toward left wrist. (Try to sustain balance in first arabesque.)

DEMI-PLIÉ IN FOURTH POSITION ÉPAULÉ—COUNT *four:* Right leg closes to fourth position front facing corner 8 with a plié à quart; that is, the right knee is bent while the left knee is straight with left foot flat on the floor. The right shoulder is turned front so that the back is partially toward the audience. Look over right shoulder and incline the head to the right épaulé. The arms are in fourth arabesque position, right arm extended in front of body to corner 8 while the left arm extends back to corner 4.

GLISSADE; DEMI-GRAND ROND DE JAMBE EN DEDANS WITH REVELÉ
—COUNT *and, five:* Same as count *and, one.*

DEMI-PLIÉ IN FOURTH POSITION CROISÉ—COUNT *six:* Same as count *two.*

STEP OVER AND PIQUÉ INTO FIRST ARABESQUE—COUNT *and, seven:* Same as count *and, three.*

DEMI-PLIÉ IN FOURTH POSITION ÉPAULÉ—COUNT *eight:* Same as count *four.*

TWO

This combination continues to move on a diagonal to corner 8.

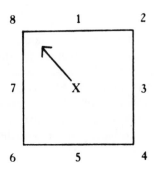

Repeat combination ONE through count *and, seven.* Continue as follows:

FONDU IN FIRST ARABESQUE—COUNT *eight:* After last piqué arabesque, demi-plié on left leg while right leg remains extended back. Arms remain in first arabesque position with left arm front. Body and head face corner 8.

THREE

This combination moves backward on a slight diagonal toward side 3.

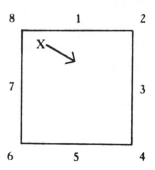

GLISSADE EN ARRIÈRE—COUNT *and:* Glissade backward starting with right foot in direction of side 3, and open right foot dégagé back with a demi-plié on the left foot. Arms move downward to preparatory position. Body and head are facing corner 8.

PIQUÉ BACK ON RIGHT POINTE INTO ARABESQUE CROISÉE—COUNT *one:* Piqué onto the right pointe, at the same time passing left leg through first position and raising it back in arabesque croisée. Right elbow bends, bringing right palm toward the lips, and then opens outward and forward toward the audience; left arm is in second position. Shoulders turn slightly front to face audience; look toward audience on the port-de-bras.

PIQUÉ BACK ON LEFT POINTE INTO ARABESQUE EFFACÉE—COUNT *two:* Fondu (demi-plié) on right foot and piqué back onto the left pointe, at the same time passing right leg through first position and raising it back in arabesque effacée. Arms pass through first position en avant to first arabesque position with the left arm front. Head is in profile looking toward left wrist. Body faces corner 8.

PIQUÉ TOUR EN DEDANS WITH LEFT FOOT FRONT IN RETIRÉ—COUNT
and, three: Demi-plié quickly on left foot while the right leg
turns on the pivot of its hip into dégagé front effacé toward
the right (side 3). Put a strong impetus on the demi-plié so
that there is enough force for the piqué tour en dedans on right
pointe; bring the left foot retiré in front of right knee; step to
corner 4. Execute a turn and a half-turn en dedans, spotting
to upstage corner 4 during the one turn; then spot quickly to
downstage left corner 8 for the last half-turn. The right arm
moves strongly to second position from first position front while
the left arm is in second position, and then both arms move
upward through second position into third position en haut.

POINTE TENDUE À TERRE EFFACÉE WITH LEFT FOOT—COUNT
four: After piqué tour en dedans finish in fourth position
with left foot pointe tendue à terre effacée front with a demi-plié
on right foot, facing downstage corner 8. Look toward left foot
as body inclines toward left foot. Arms open quickly downward
through first position and move outward and back, extended in
low second position with palms up slightly and facing downward.

PIQUÉ BACK ON RIGHT POINTE INTO ARABESQUE CROISÉE—COUNT *and,*
five:. Instead of glissade en arrière, dégagé right foot to back
on count *and,* and repeat count *one.*

PIQUÉ BACK ON LEFT POINTE INTO ARABESQUE EFFACÉE—COUNT
six: Same as count *two.*

PIQUÉ TOUR EN DEDANS WITH LEFT FOOT FRONT IN RETIRÉ—COUNT
and, seven: Same as count *and, three.*

POINTE TENDUE À TERRE EFFACÉE WITH LEFT FOOT—COUNT
eight: Same as count *four.*

FOUR

---

*This combination continues to move backward
on slight diagonal to side 3.*

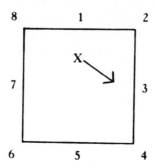

Repeat combination THREE, but omit glissade and start with dégagé to side.

FIVE

This combination moves sideways toward corner 6.

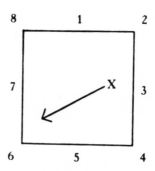

BRING LEFT FOOT TO FIFTH POSITION BACK—ANTICIPATE THE

MUSIC: From pointe tendue effacée à terre with right foot in demi-plié, bring left foot behind right foot in fifth position demi-plié. The right arm moves to first position en avant; left arm to second position. Body inclines to the right side; look over the right shoulder toward right arm.

PAS DE BOURRÉE COURU TO THE SIDE IN FIFTH POSITION AND RETIRÉ LEFT FOOT BACK OF RIGHT KNEE—COUNT *and, one:* Step on left pointe to left side toward upstage corner 6, at the same time rising up on right pointe and bringing the right foot front so that feet are in fifth position sur les pointes. Execute two bourrées sideways toward upstage corner 6. Then, remaining sur la pointe on right foot, bend the right knee slightly and raise left foot retiré to back of right knee. Arms remain low (at hip level) as they both move toward left side with a graceful movement until they extend to left side. Body and head incline to right side; look over right shoulder and arm.

PAS DE BOURRÉE COURU TO THE SIDE IN FIFTH POSITION AND RETIRÉ RIGHT FOOT IN FRONT OF LEFT KNEE—COUNT *and, two:* Remaining sur les pointes, return left foot to fifth position back and execute two bourrées sideways toward upstage left corner 6. Then, remaining sur la pointe on left foot, bend the left knee slightly and raise right foot retiré to front of left knee. Arms remain low (at hip level) as they both move toward right with a graceful movement until they extend to the right side. Body and head incline to left side; look over left shoulder and arm.

PAS DE BOURRÉE COURU TO THE SIDE IN FIFTH POSITION AND RETIRÉ LEFT FOOT BACK OF RIGHT KNEE—COUNT *and, three:* Same as count *and, one.*

PAS DE BOURRÉE COURU TO THE SIDE IN FIFTH POSITION AND RETIRÉ RIGHT FOOT FRONT OF LEFT KNEE—COUNT *and, four:* Same count *and, two.*

PAS DE BOURRÉE COURU TO THE SIDE IN FIFTH POSITION—COUNT: *and five, and six, and seven, and eight:* Remaining sur la pointe on left foot, return right foot to fifth position sur les pointes front and bourrée sideways to upstage corner 6 with eight tiny steps in fifth position sur les pointes, stopping at upstage corner 6 in fifth position sur les pointes, with right foot front croisé. Arms move with a sweeping movement from right side downward and then move upward toward left side remaining parallel to each other. They continue upward to third position

en haut and are held in a rounded position at upstage left corner
6. Head follows movement of arms from right to left, then faces
front and inclines to the right as arms reach third position en
haut. Body inclines from right side to left side and then straightens
while following movement of arms; right shoulder is brought
slightly forward.

SIX*

This combination moves forward on a diagonal toward corner 2.

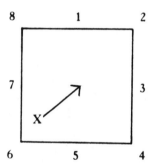

Demi-plié in fifth position effacé—anticipate the music.
Come down from fifth position sur les pointes into demi-plié in
fifth position (right foot front) facing corner 2. Arms move
downward while extending forward parallel to each other, passing through first position. Body faces downstage corner 2; look
toward arms.

Sissonne fermée en avant—count *and, one:* Jump forward and
upward from right foot, at the same time quickly raising left foot
back with straight knee, closing into fifth position back demi-plié.
Continue facing corner 2. Both arms extend front, right arm
slightly higher than the left arm. Elbows should not be too rigid
but should gracefully relax and straighten during movement;
palms face downward. Body remains facing downstage corner 2.
Look toward arms, inclining head slightly to the right.

* *For a slightly different version, see notes following this variation.*

Sissonne ouverte en avant

Sissonne ouverte en avant—count *two:* Jump forward again on right foot toward downstage corner 2, raising left foot back with straight knee, and come down in demi-plié on right foot while left foot remains extended back in arabesque effacée. Arms remain extended front, same as before. Body and head remain the same.

Pas de bourrée piqué changée—count *and, three:* Draw left leg to back of right foot on the floor, at the same time rising sur les pointes in fifth position. Immediately raise right foot to front of left knee; step on right pointe to second position remaining sur les pointes; bring left foot quickly to front of right knee and drop left foot forward into fourth position demi-plié, with the weight of the body equally on both legs, as a preparation for the following pirouette. Arms open to second position during pas de bourrée with right arm moving front to third arabesque position with palm down; left arm remains in second position, in preparation for the pirouette.

DOUBLE PIROUETTE EN DEHORS ENDING IN FIFTH POSITION—COUNT *four:* Raise right foot to retiré front with relevé on left pointe as body turns to right during double turns. The timing of the arms is this: first right arm opens with force and then left arm rises upward with force to meet right arm en haut. Head spots twice to downstage corner 2.

—The pirouette closes in demi-plié fifth position effacé with right foot front. Both arms move downward from third position en haut to first position en avant with a quick movement. Body remains facing corner 2.

SISSONNE FERMÉE EN AVANT—COUNT *and, five:* Same as count *and, one.*

SISSONNE OUVERTE EN AVANT—COUNT *six:* Same as count *two.*

PAS DE BOURRÉE PIQUÉ CHANGÉE—COUNT *and, seven:* Same as count *and, three.*

DOUBLE PIROUETTE EN DEHORS ENDING IN FIFTH POSITION—COUNT *eight:* Same as count *four.*

SEVEN

This combination continues on the diagonal to corner 2 and then moves left toward side 7.

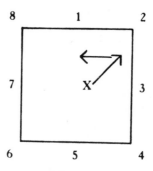

SISSONNE FERMÉE EN AVANT—COUNT *and, one:* Same as combination SIX—count *and, one.*

SISSONNE OUVERTE EN AVANT—COUNT *two:* Same as combination
SIX—count *two.*

PAS DE BOURRÉE PIQUÉ CHANGÉE—COUNT *and, three:* Same as combination SIX—count *and, three.*

DOUBLE PIROUETTE EN DEHORS ENDING WITH LEFT FOOT SUR LE
COU-DE-PIED BACK—COUNT *four:* After pirouettes, come down
in demi-plié on right foot and raise left foot back sur le cou-de-
pied croisé. (Arms are in third position on turns.) After the turns
arms open from third position en haut outward to second position; the right arm bends front in first position en avant while
left arm remains in second position. Body inclines to the right;
look over right shoulder at right arm.

PIQUÉ EN ARRIÈRE WITH RIGHT FOOT RETIRÉ FRONT—COUNT *and,*
five: Dégagé left foot to back and piqué sur la pointe toward
side 7, at the same time bringing right foot to front of left knee.
Arms, head, and body remain the same.

PIQUÉ EN ARRIÈRE WITH RIGHT FOOT RETIRÉ FRONT—COUNT
six: Demi-plié on right foot front bringing left foot sur le
cou-de-pied back and repeat count *and, five,* moving left toward
side 7.

DEMI-PLIÉ ON LEFT FOOT RAISING RIGHT FOOT FRONT IN LOW HALF-
BENT POSITION—COUNT *and:* Come down in demi-plié back on
left foot, at the same time raising right foot low front croisé with
knee bent. Right arm remains front in first position, with left
arm in second position. Body is facing downstage corner 8; look
toward audience over right shoulder.

EMBOÎTÉ RAISING LEFT FOOT FRONT IN LOW HALF-BENT POSITION—
COUNT *seven:* Jump up on left foot turning to the left so that
body faces downstage corner 2 and come down on right foot in
demi-plié, at the same time raising left foot front with bent knee
in croisé. (The back faces audience for a moment during the
jump.) The left arm moves to first position en avant and the
right arm opens to second position. Look toward downstage
corner 2.

PETIT ASSEMBLÉ EN AVANT WITH LEFT FOOT CROISÉ AND SOUS-SUS
SUR LES POINTES—COUNT *and, eight:* Jump up on right foot at
the same time thrusting left foot front croisé toward downstage

corner 2 while straightening left knee. Come down in fifth position with left foot front croisé in demi-plié and quickly relevé sur les pointes in fifth position croisé with left foot still in front. Arms pass through first position en avant and rise en haut to third position. Body and head face toward audience.

EIGHT†

This combination moves slightly toward side 7 at center stage into the final pose.

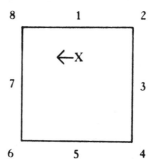

There is a pause in the music before the final combination.

REMAIN STANDING SUR LES POINTES in fifth position left foot front croisé. Arms remain en haut in third position well rounded. Look toward audience.

FAILLI INTO FOURTH POSITION DEMI-PLIÉ—COUNT *and:* Quickly demi-plié in fifth position and spring off both feet moving to the left (side 7), changing épaulement so that right shoulder comes forward, while the right foot rises back in effacé (45°) and comes down in fourth position front croisé demi-plié. Quickly raise left foot back sur le cou-de-pied. Both arms open to second position (anticipate the movement by opening a little before the music) and the palms turn downward on the épaulement so that arms are in first arabesque position. Body faces downstage corner 8; look toward side 7.

† *For a slightly different version, see notes following this variation.*

PIQUÉ ARABESQUE EFFACÉE—COUNT *one:* Quickly step on the left
pointe to side 7, raising right foot back, and immediately come
down off left pointe without demi-plié and lower right foot to
pointe tendue effacée back à terre. Arms remain in first arabesque position. Body faces left toward side 7; look toward left
wrist.

HOLD POSITION WITH POINTE TENDUE RIGHT FOOT EFFACÉ BACK—
COUNT *two:* Hold pointe tendue right foot effacé back position
as the body inclines slightly back and head and shoulders turn
slightly toward audience. The left arm rises en haut with palm
turned outward and the right arm lowers with palm raised
slightly and turned downward. (This is a version of first
arabesque position.)

Notes

There are slightly different versions of some details of the Lilac Fairy variation. Following are some of these details:

ONE

DEMI-GRAND ROND DE JAMBE EN DEDANS WITH RELEVÉ—COUNT *one:* The rond de jambe may begin with a développé with left leg instead of a rising into relevé with the leg straight.

SIX

SISSONNE OUVERTE EN AVANT—COUNT *two:* May be changed from ouverte to fermée with demi-plié in fifth position.

PAS DE BOURRÉE PIQUÉ CHANGÉE—COUNT *and, three:* May become relevé-retiré front with right foot rising to front of left knee and returning fifth front demi-plié.

DOUBLE PIROUETTE EN DEHORS—COUNT *four:* Double pirouette may be taken from fifth position with right foot front and returning to fifth position demi-plié with right foot front.

EIGHT

FAILLI INTO FOURTH POSITION DEMI-PLIÉ—COUNT *and:* May become piqué into first arabesque on right pointe raising left foot back. Close left foot fourth position front demi-plié in preparation for following pirouette.

Piqué arabesque effacée—count *one:* This may become a double pirouette en dehors on left pointe, right foot retiré front.

Hold position with pointe tendue right foot effacé back—count *two:* After the pirouettes, the final pose may be changed as follows. Finish down in fourth position right foot back croisé with the right knee on the floor and the left foot front flat on the floor, with knee bent.

PAS DE QUATRE INTRADA
PART ONE

From the Ballet

The Sleeping Beauty

La Belle au Bois Dormant

PAS DE QUATRE INTRADA
PART ONE

This variation is danced by three soloists in unison during their entrance in the first Pas de Quatre in Act III and is the first part of a two-part variation. (The second pas de quatre is now known as the Bluebird pas de deux.) MUSIC by Peter Ilyich Tchaikovsky. CHOREOGRAPHY by Marius Petipa. AS TAUGHT by Ludmilla Shollar and Anatole Vilzak. NOTATED by Laurencia Klaja. TEMPO 6/8, allegro non tanto.

Recommended Recordings

1. *Tchaikovsky. Sleeping Beauty. Complete Ballet.* Conducted by André Previn, with the London Symphony Orchestra. Angel Records, SCLX 3812. Side 5, band 2, Intrada.

2. *The Sleeping Beauty Ballet. Complete.* Richard Bonynge, conductor, with the National Philharmonic Orchestra. London Records, London FFRR, CSA 2316. Side 5, Act III, the Pas de Quatre follows the Polacca.

Piano Music

Complete Piano Music for The Sleeping Beauty Ballet, by Peter Ilyich Tchaikovsky. The Intrada, page 161, is the entrance dance of a pas de quatre which is followed by solo variations for each of the four fairies and a coda. Published by The Tschaikovsky Foundation, 1950.

Comments

The Intrada, or small overture, brings the four fairies Gold, Silver, Sapphire, and Diamond on stage to join in the celebration of the marriage of Princess Aurora to Prince Florimund in Act III of the ballet. They appear first in a group of three to dance Part One and then, following without a pause after their exit, the remaining fairy appears in a solo entrance to dance Part Two of the Intrada. (Part Two is followed by solo variations for each of the fairies.)

The Intrada is choreographed as a double variation using more or less the same music for both parts, but contrasting the timing so that the first part shows off quick, jumping movements with batterie, while the second part shows off the slow balances and fast turns of the soloist. Part One is longer than Part Two by eight counts. Each part is notated here as a separate variation.

In the Diaghilev production, the Pas de Quatre was changed into a Pas de Trois for Florestan and his two sisters, choreographed by Bronislava Nijinska, sister of Vaslav Nijinsky. The original Petipa choreography used as a basis for the Diamond and Silver Fairy variations were danced in turn by each of the two sisters. Britain's Royal Ballet continues to use the Pas de Trois version instead of the original Pas de Quatre in their production. In his production, Rudolf Nureyev choreographed a Pas de Cinq for a male dancer and four fairies— Diamond, Silver, Gold, and Emerald. The first part of the double variation of the Intrada in Nureyev's production is almost identical to the one taught by Madame Shollar, although the second part becomes a pas de deux danced by the Diamond fairy and her cavalier.

INTRODUCTION

Stand at upstage right corner 4.

Count *and, one* through *and, five:* The variation begins immediately after count five. Stand with left leg pointe tendue back croisé. Both arms are extended parallel to each other at hip level to the right side toward corner 2, with left arm across the front of the body. The palms of both hands face upward and are parallel to each other. Head faces right to corner 2.

ONE

This combination moves diagonally toward corner 8.

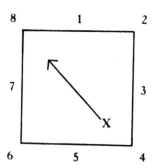

Step forward into fourth position—count *and, one:* Slide the left foot forward to corner 8 passing through first position into fourth position effacé with demi-plié, the weight forward on the left foot. Arms remain parallel to each other as they extend to the right side at hip level with a graceful movement of the wrists, with the palms now facing downward. Body and head incline to the left.

Pas de papillon
(butterfly step)

PAS DE PAPILLON (BUTTERFLY STEP)—COUNT *and, two:* Jump off the left foot in place, raising the right leg back en l'air with the knee bent as in attitude position, and come down on the right foot front after the legs have passed each other in the air with knees slightly bent back as in attitude back. The left leg is now back dégagé en l'air in attitude back croisé with a demi-plié on the right foot. The arms continue the port-de-bras started above, with both arms as a unit circling around to the left, rising to third position rounded en haut, and then circling downward to the right side, still remaining parallel to each other. Body and head follow the movement of the arms, first inclining to the left, then circling up and inclining back when both arms are in third position en haut, and finishing with the body and head inclining to the right. This circling movement of port-de-bras continues without pause during the whole combination.

CHASSÉ FORWARD INTO FOURTH POSITION—COUNT *and, three:* Slide the left foot forward to corner 8 passing through first position with a slight spring, finishing in demi-plié fourth position effacé with the left foot front. Arms pass the front of the body remaining parallel and extend to the left side at hip level with a graceful movement of the wrists, with the palms facing downward. Body and head incline to the left.

PAS DE PAPILLON (BUTTERFLY STEP)—COUNT *and, four:* Same as count *and, two.*

CHASSÉ FORWARD INTO FOURTH POSITION—COUNT *and, five:* Same as count *and, three.*

PAS DE PAPILLON (BUTTERFLY STEP)—COUNT *and, six:* Same as count *and, two.*

CHASSÉ FORWARD INTO FOURTH POSITION—COUNT *and, seven:* Same as count *and, three.*

CABRIOLE DERRIÈRE EFFACÉE—COUNT *and, eight:* From fourth position effacé with left foot front, raise the right foot dégagé back in the air (45°) and, with a strong plié, jump off the left foot and beat it under the right leg, which is in the air, coming down on the left foot again in demi-plié with right leg remaining dégagé back in the air. Arms pass through first position en avant to first arabesque position with the left arm front. Body inclines slightly back; look toward the left wrist.

TWO

*This combination moves right to side 3, and then moves around
to the left, finishing at center stage facing front.*

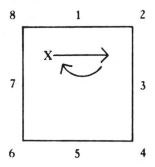

SISSONNE TOMBÉE—COUNT *and, one:*   Bend the right knee and, with
a small rond de jambe en l'air $(45°)$, change the direction of the
body to face front, at the same time jumping up off the left foot.
Then tombé forward toward side 3 onto the right foot front in
fourth position effacé in demi-plié. The right arm moves up to
first position and forward with palm up as the left arm stays in
second position. Body inclines slightly forward on tombé to side 3.
Look over the right arm.

TEMPS LEVÉ IN SECOND ARABESQUE POSITION—COUNT *and,
two:*   Transfer weight to the right foot at the same time bringing the left foot croisé back so that body faces corner 8 with the
left foot behind the right foot in fourth position croisé demi-plié.
Brush the right leg through first position into dégagé effacé with
demi-plié on the left foot, and jump off the left foot in place,
raising the right leg into arabesque back effacé. Finish with plié
on the left foot with right leg dégagé back effacé in second
arabesque position. The right arm opens forward to second position and then sweeps downward and forward into second arabesque position with the right arm front; left arm is in second
position. Body and head change direction to face side 7. Head is
inclined slightly to the right.

CHASSÉ BACK—COUNT *and, three:* Slide back on the right foot in chassé, bringing the left foot to the right foot in fifth position with a small jump, coming down on left foot in demi-plié with right foot dégagé back effacé. The right arm moves downward to meet the left arm in preparatory position. Body and head face side 7. Head inclines to the left.

JETÉ EN TOURNANT (ENTRELACÉ)—COUNT *and, four:* Step back on the right foot in demi-plié while turning to face side 3. Thrust the left foot forward en l'air to side 3, jumping up off the right foot and turning body to the right in the air in a half-turn, with legs meeting in the air, before coming down on the left foot front demi-plié with the right leg back dégagé effacé, facing side 7 again. Both arms pass through first position en avant to third position en haut rounded and open outward to first arabesque position with left arm front. Body and head face side 3 and then change to face 7.

SISSONNE TOMBÉE—COUNT *and, five:* Same as count *and, one.*

COUPÉ BALLONNÉ SAUTÉ BATTU—COUNT *and, six:* From fourth position effacé with right foot front, coupé by stepping left foot behind right foot into fifth position demi-plié. The right arm opens to wide first position front with palm upward; left arm remains in second position. Then both arms move downward to preparatory position. Body and head face front.

—Brush right leg to low second position in the air at the same time springing off the left foot and bringing it under the right calf, beating the calves together in the air, and coming down with the right foot back sur le cou-de-pied croisé. The right arm opens to second position while the left arm remains in first position en avant. Body first faces front when in the air and comes down facing corner 2 with the head inclining to the left. Look over the left arm.

SISSONNE TOMBÉE BACK, STEP-COUPÉ BACK—COUNT *and, seven:* With the right foot sur le cou-de-pied back, jump up off the left foot with temps levé and step back coupé turning around to the right with the right foot stepping forward toward the back. With the left foot step over in front of the right foot, changing the direction of the body to face side 7. Arms are in first position en avant. Look in the direction the body is going, facing corner 8.

BRISÉ DESSUS—COUNT *and, eight:*   Step forward toward corner 8 onto the right foot in demi-plié and brush the left foot to the side in low second position in the air. Springing upward and sideways off the right foot, thrust it behind the left calf and beat the calves together before alighting with the right foot front in fifth position demi-plié. The left arm remains front in first position en avant while the right arm opens to second position. Body and head face corner 8.

THREE

This combination first remains in place, moves toward side 3, and then toward side 7.

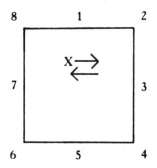

ENTRECHAT-QUATRE—COUNT *and, one:*   From fifth position with right foot front, jump into the air off both feet opening the legs slightly and beat the calves together with the left foot in front, coming down into fifth position demi-plié without changing feet, that is, with the right foot front. Arms are in preparatory position en bas at the sides with elbows rounded. Body and head face audience.

RELEVÉ PASSÉ EN ARRIÈRE—COUNT *and, two:*   Spring up onto the left pointe, at the same time raising the right foot to the side of the left knee, and on the way down pass the right leg back to fifth position demi-plié. Arms rise to first position en avant before the right arm continues upward to third position en haut as left arm opens to second position. Body and head face audience with right shoulder back.

ENTRECHAT-QUATRE—COUNT *and, three:* From fifth position with the left foot front, jump into the air off both feet, opening the legs slightly, and beat the calves together with the right foot in front, coming down into fifth position demi-plié without changing feet; that is, with the left foot front. Arms are in preparatory position en bas at the sides with elbows rounded. Body and head face audience.

RELEVÉ PASSÉ EN ARRIÈRE—COUNT *and, four:* Spring up onto the right pointe at the same time raising the left foot to the side of the right knee and on the way down pass the left leg back to fifth position demi-plié. Arms rise to first position en avant before the left arm continues upward to third position en haut and the right arm opens to second position. Body and head face audience, with the left shoulder back.

GLISSADE DEVANT—COUNT *and, five:* Remain in demi-plié on the left foot and slide the right foot to the side to second position à terre. Transfer weight to the right foot with a slight spring on the left foot and close left foot back in fifth position demi-plié. (Do not change feet.) The right arm opens outward passing through second position and down to meet the left arm in preparatory position. Body faces front; look toward corner 2.

JETÉ DESSOUS BATTU—COUNT *and, six:* With a strong plié on the left foot, thrust the right leg into low second position en l'air and, with the legs straight, jump off the left foot, bringing the left leg behind the right leg, and beat the calves together, coming down in demi-plié on the right foot with the left foot sur le cou-de-pied front. Arms rise to first position en avant. The right arm continues upward to third position rounded en haut as the left arm opens to second position. Body inclines to the right facing front. Head turns right toward corner 2.

GLISSADE DEVANT—COUNT *and, seven:* Remain in demi-plié on the right foot and slide the left foot to the side to second position à terre. Transfer weight to the left foot with a slight spring on the right foot and close right foot back in fifth position demi-plié. (Do not change feet.) The right arm opens outward passing through second position and meets the left arm in preparatory position. Body faces front. Look toward corner 8.

ASSEMBLÉ DESSOUS BATTU—COUNT *and, eight:* With a strong demi-plié on the right foot, brush the left leg to the side in second position in the air ($45°$) and, keeping knees straight, jump off the right foot, bringing it under the left leg, and beat the calves together before coming down in fifth position demi-plié with the right foot front. Arms pass through first position en avant and open to second position allongé with the left arm extended with palm downward slightly higher than shoulder level. Body faces front; look toward the left arm.

FOUR

This combination first remains in place, moves to corner 6, and then turns to face corner 2.

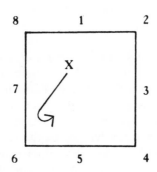

Entrechat-quatre—count *and, one:*   Same as combination three —count *and, one.*

Relevé passé en arrière—count *and, two:*   Same as combination three—count *and, two.*

Entrechat-quatre—count *and, three:* Same as combination three—count *and, three.*

Relevé passé en arrière—count *and, four:*   Same as combination three—count *and, four.*

Entrechat-quatre—count *and, five:*   Same as combination three —count *and, one.*

SISSONNE OUVERTE (BATTU)—COUNT *and, six:* (The right foot is fifth position front demi-plié.) Spring off both feet upward and sideways to the right, turning the body to the right to face side 3. Come down on the right foot in demi-plié, raising the left leg back in second arabesque position. (For battu, jump up on both feet and execute an entrechat-cinq, beating calves with the left foot front, before coming down into second arabesque position.) The left arm moves downward and sweeps forward to second arabesque position front as the right arm opens to second position. Body faces side 3. Look over the left shoulder toward the audience.

CHASSÉ BACK—COUNT *and, seven:* Slide to the back toward corner 6 on the left foot in demi-plié and with a spring draw the right foot toward the left foot. Finish in demi-plié on the right foot in the spot where the left foot was and dégagé back with left foot toward corner 6. Arms move downward to first position. Body faces corner 2. Look toward corner 2.

CABRIOLE ITALIENNE FOUETTÉE—COUNT *and, eight:* Step on the left foot with a strong demi-plié (facing toward corner 6) and brush the right leg into second position en l'air while springing up off the left foot; immediately turn on the pivot of the hip into arabesque back with the body facing corner 2. After the fouetté, and before coming down, bring the left leg to the right leg in the air with straight knees and beat the calf of the left leg under the right leg, ending with the left leg in demi-plié and the right leg extended dégagé back croisé in the air (third arabesque position). Arms pass through first position en avant. The right arm continues to allongé second position slightly higher than shoulder level with palm extended, while the right leg is in second position en l'air. As body comes down into third arabesque position, the right arm lowers front to third arabesque position with the left arm in second position. Body and head first face corner 6, turning to left to face downstage corner 2 on the third arabesque position.

FIVE

*This combination moves on the diagonal downstage from corner 6
toward corner 2, and then moves to side 3.*

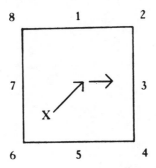

COUPÉ DÉVELOPPÉ ÉCARTÉ BACK WITH SAUTÉ—COUNT *and,
one:* Step on the right foot cutting under the left foot with a
demi-plié on the right foot, at the same time raising the left foot
sur le cou-de-pied front. Jump off the right foot and, with a
développé in écarté back to corner 6, open the left leg to second
position en l'air. Arms pass through first position en avant before
the left arm opens to third position en haut and the right arm
opens to second. Body inclines to the right. Head is turned and
inclined to right to corner 2.

PAS DE BOURRÉE DESSOUS—COUNT *and, two:* Draw left foot behind
right foot sur les demi-pointes in fifth position; with right foot
step into second position à terre sur la demi-pointe and close left
foot front in fifth position demi-plié, moving toward corner 2.
The left arm opens outward through second position and meets
the right arm in preparatory position. Body and head face front.

CABRIOLE DEVANT EFFACÉE—COUNT *and, three:* Brush the right leg
forward in effacé, at the same time jumping off the left foot and
bringing it behind the right leg with the knees straight. Beat the
left calf under the right calf, coming down on the left foot demi-
plié with the right leg extended front in effacé. Arms move to
first position en avant, with the left arm moving to third position
en haut rounded and the right arm opening to second position.
Body faces corner 2; look left.

Cabriole devant effacée

TOMBÉ, PAS DE BOURRÉE DESSOUS—COUNT *and, four:* Fall forward on the right foot in demi-plié fourth position effacé toward corner 2, with the left foot extending low dégagé back, and execute a pas de bourrée, drawing the left foot behind the right foot into fifth position sur les demi-pointes, stepping on the right demi-pointe to side in second position à terre and closing the left foot to fifth position front croisé demi-plié. The left arm opens outward to second position and then passes downward to meet the right arm in preparatory position en bas. Body faces corner 2. Look toward corner 2.

CABROILE DEVANT EFFACÉE—COUNT *and, five:* Same as count *and, three.*

TOMBÉ, PAS DE BOURRÉE DESSOUS—COUNT *and, six:* Same as count *and, four.*

GLISSADE DERRIÈRE—COUNT *and, seven:*   Slide the right foot to second position, shift the weight from the left foot to the right foot, and close the left foot fifth position front croisé in demi-plié, traveling to right (side 3). (No change in feet.) Arms open slightly to the sides in low second position. Body and head face front.

PETIT ASSEMBLÉ DESSUS—COUNT *and, eight:*   Brush the right foot to low second position en l'air (25°), at the same time jumping up off the left foot. Come down on both feet simultaneously in fifth position demi-plié effacé with right foot front. Both arms open to the sides in low second on the glissade and close to preparatory position in the fifth position demi-plié. Body first faces en face front and ends facing corner 2.

SIX

This combination moves backward from side 3 to center stage.

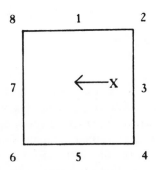

ENTRECHAT-TROIS DERRIÈRE—COUNT *and, one:*   From fifth position demi-plié, jump up off both feet opening the legs slightly and beat the right calf front over the left calf. (Both legs beat equally.) Come down on the left foot demi-plié with the right leg back sur le cou-de-pied croisé. Both arms rise to first position en avant and as the left arm opens to second position, right arm remains first position en avant. Body inclines slightly forward, facing side 3. Look over the right arm.

Coupé dessous
piqué back into arabesque

COUPÉ DESSOUS, PIQUÉ BACK INTO ARABESQUE—COUNT *and,*
two: Without straightening the right knee, step back onto the
right pointe behind the left foot, at the same time raising the left
leg back into arabesque effacée, facing side 3, and immediately
close the left leg back into fifth position effacé demi-plié. Both
arms meet in first position en avant as the left arm rises to third
position en haut rounded and the right arm opens to second
position on arabesque. In fifth position demi-plié, the left arm
has opened outward through second position to meet the right
arm in preparatory position. Head and body incline slightly back
on the arabesque and incline slightly forward on the fifth position
demi-plié. Body faces side 3.

ENTRECHAT-TROIS DERRIÈRE—COUNT *and, three:* Same as count
and, one.

COUPÉ DESSOUS, PIQUÉ BACK INTO ARABESQUE—COUNT *and, four:* Same as count *and, two.*

ENTRECHAT-TROIS DERRIÈRE—COUNT *and, five:* Same as count *and, one.*

COUPÉ DESSOUS, PIQUÉ BACK INTO ARABESQUE—COUNT *and, six:* Same as count *and, two.*

ENTRECHAT-TROIS DERRIÈRE—COUNT *and, seven:* Same as count *and, one.*

COUPÉ DESSOUS, PIQUÉ BACK INTO ARABESQUE—COUNT *and, eight* (SUSTAINED): Same as count *and, two,* except that the balance in arabesque is held slightly longer, and does not close into fifth position.

SEVEN

This combination remains in place at center stage.

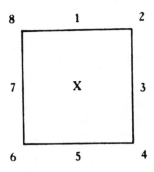

FONDU IN ARABESQUE—COUNT *and, one:* Come down in demi-plié on the right foot; left leg remains extended back in arabesque effacée facing side 3. Arms are in first arabesque position with the right arm front. Body and head face side 3.

CABRIOLE FOUETTÉE OR GRAND FOUETTÉ TO RIGHT—COUNT *and,*
two: Step forward on the left foot to side 3 and brush the
right leg forward through first position en l'air (45°). Springing
off the left foot, bring it under the right calf and beat the calves
together battu (like a cabriole front). Allowing the right leg to
turn on the pivot of the hip, turn the body left so that the right
leg is extended effacé back, then come down in demi-plié on
the left foot facing side 7 with the right leg extended back in
arabesque effacée. (By now only the strongest dancer will have
strength left for the battu, so the grand fouetté will most probably have to be substituted. In either event, do all of the series
cabriole fouettée or all grand fouetté, which is the same step but
without the battu.) Arms pass through first position en avant to
third position en haut rounded on the battu, and on the arabesque fondue, they open outward to first arabesque position with
the left arm front. Body and head first face side 3 and then finish
facing side 7.

TEMPS LEVÉ EN ARABESQUE—COUNT *and, three:* With the right leg
remaining arabesque effacée back, spring up off the left foot with
a small jump and come down in demi-plié on the left foot with
the right leg remaining extended back in arabesque effacée.
Arms are in first arabesque position with left arm front. Body
and head face side 7.

CABRIOLE FOUETTÉE OR GRAND FOUETTÉ TO LEFT—COUNT *and,*
four: Same as count *and, two,* but done to the opposite side.

TEMPS LEVÉ EN ARABESQUE—COUNT *and, five:* Same as count *and,*
three, but done to the opposite side.

CABRIOLE FOUETTÉE OR GRAND FOUETTÉ TO RIGHT—COUNT *and,*
six: Same as count *and, two.*

TEMPS LEVÉ EN ARABESQUE—COUNT *and, seven:* Same as count
and, three.

CABRIOLE FOUETTÉE OR GRAND FOUETTÉ TO LEFT—COUNT *and,*
eight: Same as count *and, two,* but done to the opposite side.

EIGHT

*This combination continues at center stage
and then moves right toward side 3.*

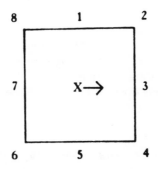

Temps levé en arabesque—count *and, one:* Same as combination seven—count *and, three,* but done to the opposite side.

Cabriole fouettée or grand fouetté to right—count *and, two:* Same as combination seven—count *and, two.*

Assemblé dessus with right leg—count *and, three:* Body is facing side 7 in demi-plié on left leg with right leg extended back in arabesque effacée. Jump off the left foot at the same time turning the right leg to second position en l'air (45°) with a turn on the pivot of the hip, closing in fifth position demi-plié with the right leg front facing en face to audience. Arms lower to preparatory position. Body and head face front en face.

Sous-sus sur les pointes—count *and, four:* Spring up with a relevé into fifth position sur place sur les pointes with right foot front croisé. Arms move to first position en avant; then the left arm opens to second position while the right arm remains in first position. Body faces front with the right shoulder slightly forward. Look toward corner 2.

CHAÎNÉS-DÉBOULÉS—COUNT *and five, and six:* With a slight turn of the body to the right and with a demi-plié on the left foot, dégagé right leg forward to side 3 and piqué onto the right pointe. With a half-turn to the right, bring left foot sur la pointe and continue turning to right while executing two chaîné-déboulé turns to the right (side 3) in first position sur les pointes. The right arm opens and then closes to meet the left arm first position en avant, where they remain during the chaînés. Head spots to side 3.

STEP-OVER—COUNT *and, seven:* Step forward to side 3 on the flat of the right foot, immediately cutting over it with the left foot into demi-plié front; bring the right foot sur le cou-de-pied back, still facing side 3. Arms open to low second position. Head and body face side 3.

PIQUÉ ARABESQUE—COUNT *and, eight:* With the left foot in demi-plié, dégagé the right foot front and piqué on the right pointe raising the left leg back in first arabesque. Arms pass through first position en avant to first arabesque position with the right arm front. Body and head face right (side 3). Look toward the right wrist.

TOMBÉ INTO FOURTH POSITION CROISÉ—COUNT *and:* From arabesque position, the left foot comes down into fourth position front croisé; the right leg goes to sur le cou-de-pied back and is released immediately to step off into the wings. The right arm moves outward and back to second position as left arm, which was in second position, sweeps backward and downward before moving forward into second arabesque position. Head looks left toward the audience as the dancer disappears into the wings just as the second variation begins from upstage right corner 4.

PAS DE QUATRE INTRADA
PART TWO

Part Two of this double variation follows the first part without a pause and is danced by the remaining soloist after the exit of the three soloists who dance Part One. This variation begins when the music starts to repeat itself a little over halfway through the Intrada. Part Two of the double variation is shorter than Part One by eight counts. It is fascinating to compare the two parts as a study in different timing to almost exactly the same music.

INTRODUCTION

Enter or stand at corner 4.

COUNT *and, five* THROUGH *and, eight:* Stand with left foot pointe tendue back croisé with leg extended. The right arm is in first position front and left arm is in second position. Body faces corner 8; look right toward the audience.

ONE

---

*This combination moves forward on a diagonal
from corner 4 toward corner 8.*

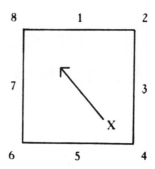

Pas couru—count *and, one:*   Step forward on the left foot toward
corner 8, and then step on the right foot with a strong demi-plié
in preparation for the following step. Arms are in low second position. Body and head face corner 8.

Grand jeté en avant—count *and, two:*   Thrust the left foot forward with a grand battement, spring forward into the air with
the right leg dégagé back effacé, and come down in first arabesque position fondu (demi-plié) on the left leg with the right
leg extended dégagé back in arabesque. Arms pass through first
position en avant to first arabesque position, with left arm front
and right arm slightly behind the shoulder line in second position.
Body faces corner 8; look toward the left wrist.

Relevé into attitude back croisé—count *and, three:*   Bring
right foot to fourth position front croisé in demi-plié passing
through first position toward corner 8. Relevé onto the right
pointe, at the same time raising the left leg back in attitude croisée with the leg halfway bent. Arms pass through preparatory position en bas to first position en avant with the right arm rising to
third position en haut rounded and the left arm opening to second position. Body faces corner 8. Head looks toward the audience.

Relevé into attitude back croisé

HOLD BALANCE IN ATTITUDE BACK CROISÉ—COUNT *and, four:*   Hold
   balance until the last moment, then fondu (demi-plié) on the
   right leg with the left leg remaining attitude back croisé, and
   proceed with the following step. Right arm opens outward to second position on the fondu. Body and head face corner 8.

PAS COURU—COUNT *and, five:*   Same as count *and, one.*

GRAND JETÉ EN AVANT—COUNT *and, six:*   Same as count *and, two.*

RELEVÉ INTO ATTITUDE BACK CROISÉ—COUNT *and, seven:*   Same as
   count *and, three.*

HOLD BALANCE IN ATTITUDE BACK CROISÉ—COUNT *and, eight:*   Same
   as count *and, four.*

TWO

---

*This combination continues the diagonal to
corner 8 and then moves to side 3.*

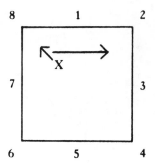

Pas couru—count *and, one:* Same as combination one—count *and, one.*

Grand jeté en avant—count *and, two:* Same as combination one—count *and, two.*

Relevé into attitude back croisé—count *and, three:* Same as combination one—count *and, three.*

Sous-sus sur les pointes—count *and, four:* (At this point the end of the diagonal has been reached at corner 8.) Close the left foot back into fifth position demi-plié and relevé sur les pointes in fifth position in place. Right arm opens outward to second position during the demi-plié and then joins the left arm in first position en avant as both arms rise to third position en haut rounded. Body faces corner 8. Head inclines slightly to the right; look front toward audience. Right shoulder is slightly forward.

Cabriole derrière effacée—count *and, five:* Step forward to side 3 in demi-plié effacé on the right foot, raise the left foot dégagé back, and execute a small cabriole back by beating the right leg under the left leg with straight knees. Both arms open outward as the right arm moves front and upward to first arabesque position. The left arm moves to second. Body faces side 3; look toward right arm.

TOMBÉ FORWARD—COUNT *and, six:*   Fall forward into fourth position
front on the left foot in demi-plié with the right foot sur le cou-
de-pied back. Arms lower to low second position at the sides.
Body and head face side 3.

RUN TO RIGHT—COUNT *and seven, and eight:*   Run toward side 3,
right foot, left foot, right foot, stopping in a pose on the right
foot front in demi-plié with the left foot sur le cou-de-pied back
effacé. The right arm moves to first position en avant; left arm
moves to second position. Body inclines toward the right side,
facing corner 2. Look over the right arm.

THREE

This combination moves backward toward side 7.

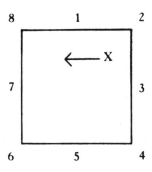

PAS DE BOURRÉE COURU EN CINQUIÈME EN ARRIÈRE—COUNT *and,
one:*   With a demi-plié on the right foot and a dégagé back
with the left foot, step back onto the left pointe toward side 7,
drawing the right pointe front into fifth position effacé sur les
pointes, and take two tiny steps sur les pointes backward toward
side 7. (The left leg with knee slightly bent leads the right leg,
which remains straight.) The right arm remains in first position
en avant; left arm remains in second position. Body straightens
and faces corner 2. Remain looking over the right arm.

Relevé-développé
à la seconde en l'air

RELEVÉ-DÉVELOPPÉ À LA SECONDE EN L'AIR—COUNT *and, two:* From
   fifth position sur les pointes with right foot front effacé, step
   in demi-plié on the left foot. Bring the right foot sur le cou-
   de-pied front, and immediately relevé onto the left pointe
   and développé the right leg to second position écarté front (over
   90°) toward corner 2. Arms pass through first position en avant
   with the right arm rising to third position rounded en haut and
   the left arm opening to second position. Body faces écarté front
   to corner 2, with right shoulder forward. Look toward corner 2.

TOMBÉ, JETÉ DESSUS RIGHT—COUNT *and, three:* From the
   développé, fall forward to the right side with a small jeté onto
   the right foot in demi-plié. Bring the left foot sur le cou-de-pied
   back. The right arm opens outward through second position and
   then both arms sway to the right side parallel to each other. Body
   and head face front.

JETÉ DESSUS LEFT, JETÉ DESSUS RIGHT—COUNT *and, four:* Brush
the left leg to low second position coming down on the left foot
in demi-plié with the right foot sur le cou-de-pied back. Both
arms sway to the left side parallel to each other. Body and head
face front.

—Brush the right leg to low second position, springing off the left
leg, and come down on the right foot in demi-plié with the left
foot sur le cou-de-pied back. Both arms sway to the right side
parallel to each other. Body and head face front.

PAS DE BOURRÉE COURU EN CINQUIÈME EN ARRIÈRE—COUNT *and, five:*
Same as count *and, one.*

RELEVÉ-DÉVELOPPÉ À LA SECONDE EN L'AIR—COUNT *and, six:* Same
as count *and, two.*

TOMBÉ, JETÉ DESSUS RIGHT—COUNT *and, seven:* Same as count
and, three.

JETÉ DESSUS LEFT, JETÉ DESSUS RIGHT—COUNT *and, eight:* Same
as count *and, four.*

FOUR

*This combination continues left to side 7
and finishes at center stage back.*

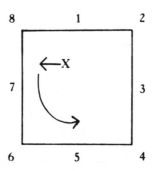

PAS DE BOURRÉE COURU EN CINQUIÈME EN ARRIÈRE—COUNT *and,*
one: Same as combination THREE—count *and, one.*

Relevé-développé à la seconde en l'air—count *and, two:* Same as combination THREE—count *and, two.*

Tombé, jeté dessus right—count *and, three:* Same as combination THREE—count *and, three.*

Jeté dessus left, jeté dessus right—count *and, four:* Same as combination THREE—count *and, four.*

Cabriole derrière—count *and, five:* Step on the left foot in demi-plié to corner 6 with right leg dégagé back and execute a small cabriole back, beating the left foot under the right foot; the back is half turned away from the audience. Arms move to first arabesque position with left arm front. Body and head face corner 6.

Tombé onto the right foot—count *and, six:* Fall forward with the weight on the right foot front in fourth position demi-plié and bring the left foot back sur le cou-de-pied. Arms lower to second position. Body and head face back.

Run around to left to center stage back—count *and, seven:* Step around to the left with left foot, run around to stage center back, and step forward to the front on the right foot. Arms are in low second position. Body and head end facing audience.

Fifth position with right foot front—count *and, eight:* Close the left foot behind right foot in fifth position flat; with knees straight, at center stage back en face. Arms are in low second position. Body and head face audience.

FIVE

This combination moves gradually forward toward the audience, at the same time moving from side to side.

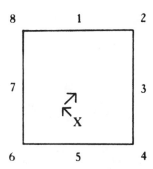

PIQUÉ EN AVANT CROISÉ—COUNT *and, one:* Demi-plié on the left
foot with a dégagé front croisé of the right leg and piqué forward
onto the right pointe toward corner 8, bringing the left foot retiré
back. Arms are gracefully crossed on the chest with the right arm
over the left arm and the elbows slightly raised away from the
body, palms facing the chest. Body faces corner 8 and inclines
slightly back. Head inclines slightly back; look to the right toward the audience.

PIQUÉ EN AVANT CROISÉ—COUNT *and, two:* Fall back onto the left
foot in demi-plié with right leg dégagé front croisé and continue
as in count *and, one.* Arms remain gracefully crossed on the chest
with the right arm over the left arm and the elbows slightly
raised away from the body, the palms facing the chest. Body
faces corner 8 and inclines slightly back. Head inclines slightly
back; look right toward the audience.

PAS DE BOURRÉE PIQUÉ DESSOUS—COUNT *and three, and
four:* Remaining sur la pointe on the right foot, close left
pointe behind right pointe, immediately raise the right foot retiré
in front of left knee, step to the right side onto the right pointe in
second position à terre while remaining on the left pointe, and
immediately raise the left foot retiré front of the right knee. Arms
rise to third position en haut rounded and then elbows straighten
and palms extend facing outward into allongé.

—Remaining sur la pointe on the right leg, close the left pointe to
front fifth position croisé sur les pointes. Arms open gradually
outward to low second position, passing into the next position
with a continuous movement. Body and head face front.

Piqué en avant croisé

PIQUÉ EN AVANT CROISÉ—COUNT *and, five:* Same as count *and, one,* but done to the opposite side.

PIQUÉ EN AVANT CROISÉ—count *and, six:* Same as count *and, two,* but done to the opposite side.

PAS DE BOURRÉE PIQUÉ DESSOUS—COUNT *and seven, and eight:* Same as count *and three, and four,* but done to the opposite side.

SIX

This combination continues moving forward, at the same time moving from side to side as before.

Pas de bourrée piqué dessous

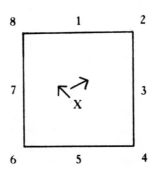

PIQUÉ EN AVANT CROISÉ—COUNT *and, one:* Same as combination
FIVE—count *and, one.*

PIQUÉ EN AVANT CROISÉ—COUNT *and, two:* Same as combination
FIVE—count *and, two.*

PAS DE BOURRÉE PIQUÉ DESSOUS—COUNT *and three, and four:* Same as combination FIVE—count *and three, and four.*

PIQUÉ EN AVANT CROISÉ—COUNT *and, five:* Same as combination FIVE—count *and, one,* but done to the opposite side.

PIQUÉ EN AVANT CROISÉ—COUNT *and, six:* Same as combination FIVE—count *and, two,* but done to the opposite side.

PAS DE BOURRÉE PIQUÉ DESSOUS—COUNT *and seven, and eight:* Same as combination FIVE—count *and three, and four,* but done to the opposite side. On count *and eight,* the right arm moves to first position en avant while the left arm moves to second position. Body faces front; look toward corner 2.

SEVEN*

This combination is a series of turns on the diagonal to corner 2.

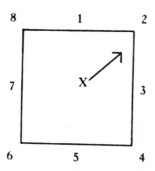

PIQUÉ TOUR EN DEHORS—COUNT *and, one:* From fifth position sur les pointes, fall forward toward corner 2 on the right foot in demi-plié with the left foot dégagé in low second position. Draw the left foot onto the left pointe in front of the right foot. At the same time raise the right foot retiré front of the left knee and turn en dehors to the right, making one complete turn to face corner 2 again. The right arm opens forward and then closes to

---

* Please note: because of the fast tempo on the recommended recording, it is best to do only two piqués tours en dehors (in half-time) instead of the choreographed four piqués tours en dehors.

meet the left arm in first position en avant on the turn. Body faces corner 2. Head spots to corner 2.

PIQUÉ TOUR EN DEHORS—COUNT *and, two:*   Same as count *and, one,* continuing on the diagonal.

PIQUÉ TOUR EN DEHORS—COUNT *and, three:*   Same as count *and, one* continuing on the diagonal.

PIQUÉ TOUR EN DEHORS—COUNT *and, four:*   Same as count *and, one,* continuing on the diagonal.

PAS DE BOURRÉE SUR PLACE EN CINQUIÈME WITH A HALF-TURN TO THE RIGHT—COUNT *and, five:*   Remaining on the left pointe after the last piqué tour en dehors, close the right foot front fifth position sur les pointes and, remaining in one spot in fifth position, bourrée with tiny steps, turning to the right to face the back. Quickly change the feet by bringing the left foot front fifth position sur les pointes. The right arm moves through first position en avant to third position rounded en haut as the left arm moves to second position. Body is now facing back and inclines to the right. Look right toward corner 6.

PAS DE BOURRÉE SUR PLACE EN CINQUIÈME WITH A HALF-TURN TO THE RIGHT—COUNT *and, six:*   Continue to bourrée to the right, now with the left foot fifth position front sur les pointes. End facing front with the left foot remaining fifth position front sur les pointes. The right arm moves gracefully outward to second position as the left arm moves gracefully through first position en avant to third position rounded en haut. Body inclines to left and is now facing front. Look left toward corner 8.

DEMI-PLIÉ IN FIFTH POSITION CROISÉ—COUNT *and, seven:*   Demi-plié in fifth position croisé with the left foot front. The left arm opens gracefully to second position and then both arms close to preparatory position en bas. Body faces corner 2; look toward corner 2.

RELEVÉ ATTITUDE FRONT CROISÉ—COUNT *and, eight:*   From fifth position croisé demi-plié, relevé onto the right pointe, at the same time raising left foot to attitude front croisé, with leg halfway bent. Arms pass through first position en avant as the right arm continues to third position rounded en haut and the left arm opens to second position. Body faces croisé to corner 2; look front toward the audience.

GOLD FAIRY
VARIATION

From the Ballet

The Sleeping Beauty

La Belle au Bois Dormant

GOLD FAIRY VARIATION

This is Variation I of the first Pas de Quatre in Act III of *The Sleeping Beauty* ballet and is danced by a soloist. MUSIC by Peter Ilyich Tchaikovsky. CHOREOGRAPHY by Marius Petipa. As TAUGHT by Anatole Vilzak. NOTATED by Laurencia Klaja. TEMPO 3/4, allegro (tempo di valse).

Recommended Recording

The Sleeping Beauty Ballet. Complete. Richard Bonynge, conductor, with the National Philharmonic Orchestra. London Records, London FFRR, CSA 2316. Side 5, Act III, the Gold Fairy variation directly follows the Pas de Quatre (Intrada).

Piano Music

Complete Piano Music for The Sleeping Beauty Ballet, by Peter Ilyich Tchaikovsky. Variation I, Waltz, page 163. Published by The Tschaikovsky Foundation, 1950.

Comments

This solo variation follows immediately after the two variations of the Intrada, or entrance, for the Pas de Quatre, which have been notated in the two preceding chapters.

The most distinguishing feature of the Gold Fairy variation is a series of relevés ballonnés fondus moving forward en face on alternate legs. Since this variation, like the Sapphire Fairy variation, is sometimes omitted in full-length productions of the ballet, the relevé ballonné fondu series may appear in the Vision Scene of Act II, where it is danced by Princess Aurora with a slow, controlled movement very beautiful to behold. Rudolf Nureyev, in his production, has transferred the music for the Gold Fairy to the same Act II Vision Scene as a solo for the Prince that begins with the same series of relevés ballonnés fondus.

According to Anatole Vilzak, when the Pas de Quatre was being transformed into a Pas de Trois by Alexander Gorsky, a ballet director and choreographer of the Maryinsky Theatre and the Bolshoi Theatre around the turn of the century, this Gold Fairy variation was added to the Act II Vision Scene and danced by Princess Aurora.

INTRODUCTION

Stand at the back of center stage.

COUNT *one* THROUGH *four:* Stand with right leg pointe tendue croisé back. Make a révérence by bending forward toward the audience with a demi-plié on the left leg while bringing the right foot sur le cou-de-pied back. Temps lié back onto the right foot to demi-plié in fourth position. Pointe tendue croisé front with the left leg and straighten the right knee with the right foot remaining flat on the floor. Both arms move outward and upward to third position en haut as the body and head incline to the left.

ONE

*This combination moves straight forward
from the back toward the front.*

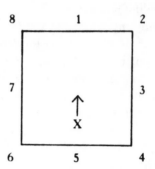

RELEVÉ À LA SECONDE—COUNT *and, one:* Transfer weight forward onto the left foot in demi-plié and relevé onto the left pointe, at the same time raising the right leg à la seconde en l'air (90° or over) écarté to corner 2. Arms open outward and/or downward, then passing through first position arms rise to second position extended allongé with the right arm slightly higher, palms extended and facing downward. Right shoulder is forward in écarté. Look toward corner 2.

BALLONNÉ—COUNT *two:* Remaining sur la pointe on left leg, bend the right knee and bring the right foot in front of the left knee. Immediately fondu on the left leg in demi-plié with right foot sur le cou-de-pied front, changing the direction of the body to face corner 8. Open the right foot in fourth position front croise and demi-plié on both feet with a smooth, flowing movement. Bend the right elbow and bring the right palm toward chest in a vertical position with palm facing the left side. Then gracefully push the raised palm forward; left arm remains in second position. Right shoulder moves forward with the motion of the right arm so that the body faces corner 8. Look slightly to the right toward the audience.

RELEVÉ À LA SECONDE—COUNT *and, three:* Same as count *and, one,* but done to the opposite side.

BALLONNÉ—COUNT *four:* Same as count *two,* but done to the opposite side.

RELEVÉ À LA SECONDE—COUNT *and, five:* Same as count *and, one.*

BALLONNÉ—COUNT *six:* Same as count *two.*

RELEVÉ À LA SECONDE—COUNT *and, seven:* Same as count *and, one,* but done to the opposite side.

BALLONNÉ—COUNT *eight:* Same as count *two,* but done to the opposite side.

TWO

This combination continues moving forward and ends with a walk to corner 6.

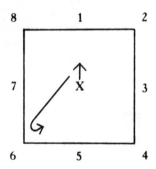

RELEVÉ À LA SECONDE—COUNT *and, one:* Same as combination ONE—count *and, one.*

BALLONNÉ—COUNT *two:* Same as combination ONE—count *two.*

TEMPS LIÉ—COUNT *and, three:* In a continuous, smooth movement, from fourth position with right foot front croisé, pointe tendue left foot back croisé and close left foot back into fifth position demi-plié. Arms move to preparatory position at the sides. Body and head face corner 8.

Sous-sus sur les pointes—count *four:* Relevé in place on both
feet in fifth position croisé sur les pointes. Arms rise to third position en haut rounded. Right shoulder is forward; look toward
audience.

Walk gracefully to corner 6—count *and five, and six, and
seven:* Step to the left with the left foot and walk gracefully
sur les demi-pointes around to the left toward corner 6, left foot,
right foot, left foot, right foot, left foot, right foot. Arms are in
low second position at the sides. Body faces toward corner 6.
Look toward corner 6.

Change direction of body to face front—count *and, eight:* As
soon as corner 6 is reached, step forward onto the left foot, at the
same time turning the body to the left so that it faces front toward audience. Immediately close the right foot back into fifth
position flat with knees straight. Arms are in low second position.
Body and head face audience.

THREE

*This combination moves on a diagonal from corner 6 toward
corner 2.*

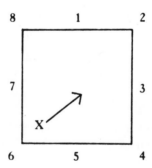

Glissade pressée—count *and:* Demi-plié in fifth position and,
with a short, quick movement, glissade to the right side toward
corner 2 without changing the feet. The right arm moves to first
position en avant as left arm moves to second position. Body
faces front; look toward corner 2.

PIQUÉ TOUR EN DEDANS—COUNT *one:* Demi-plié on the left foot and, with a dégagé of the right foot, step to the right onto the right pointe and, bringing the left foot retiré behind the right knee, execute a turn to the right on right pointe. The right arm opens, then both arms rise to third position en haut passing through second position. Head spots to corner 2.

POINTE TENDUE CROISÉE—COUNT *two:* Finish the turn with a demi-plié on the right foot and a pointe tendue front croisé with the left foot. Arms move downward in front of the body and open backward, so that both arms are stretched behind the body in low second position. Body inclines forward toward the left foot. With the chin raised, look toward the left foot. Body faces corner 2.

BALLOTTÉ—COUNT *and:* Step forward onto the left foot in demi-plié and spring into the air off both feet, at the same time passing the right foot through sur le cou-de-pied back to open to second position en l'air (45°) écarté toward corner 2. Come down on the left leg in demi-plié with the right leg in second position in the air. Arms are in second position. Body faces front; look toward corner 2.

BALLONNÉ—COUNT *three:* Jump up on the left foot with the right foot extended in dégagé second position in the air. Come down on the left foot in demi-plié as the right knee bends and the right foot goes to sur le cou-de-pied back. (This may also be done with a battu as both calves beat together with the right foot front before coming down on the left foot demi-plié with right foot sur le cou-de-pied back.) The right arm moves to first position en avant; left arm remains in second position. Look toward corner 2.

PAS DE CHAT—COUNT *four:* From demi-plié on the left foot, jump sideways to the right toward corner 2 with both knees bent in the air. Come down first on the right foot, then the left foot, in fifth position demi-plié with the left foot front. The left arm moves upward from second position to third position en haut while the right arm remains in first position en avant. Body is straight. Look toward corner 2.

GLISSADE PRESSÉE; PIQUÉ TOUR EN DEDANS—COUNT *and, five:* Same as count *and, one.*

POINTE TENDUE CROISÉE—COUNT *six:* Same as count *two.*

Ballotté; ballonné—count *and, seven:* Same as count *and, three.*

Pas de chat—count *eight:* Same as count *four.*

FOUR

This combination continues the diagonal toward corner 2, then moves to side 7.

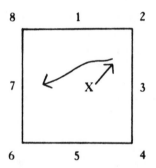

Glissade pressée, piqué tour en dedans—count *and, one:* Same as combination three—count *and, one.*

Pointe tendue croisée—count *two:* Same as combination three —count *two.*

Fifth position demi-plié—count *and:* Remaining in demi-plié on the left leg, close the left foot to fifth position front demi-plié croisé. Arms move to preparatory position. Body straightens. Head and body face corner 2.

Sous-sus sur les pointes—count *three, four:* Relevé onto both feet in fifth position sur les pointes. Arms pass through first position to third position en haut rounded. Body faces corner 2 and inclines slightly to the left. Look toward the audience.

Walk to left toward side 7—count *and five, and six, and seven:* Facing front, step to the left with the left foot and walk gracefully sur les demi-pointes straight toward side 7, left foot, right foot, left foot, right foot, left foot, right foot. Arms open outward on first step and move to low second position. Head and body face side 7.

POINTE TENDUE CROISÉE—COUNT *and, eight:* Step to the side on the left foot, so that the body faces front, and bring the right foot pointe tendue front croisé in preparation for the following combination. The right arm moves to first position en avant; left arm moves to second position. Body faces front. Look toward corner 2.

FIVE

This combination moves straight to side 3.

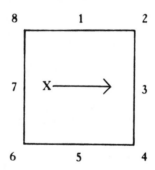

SAUT DE BASQUE—COUNT *and, one, two* (SLOW TEMPO): Step to the side toward side 3 on the right foot in demi-plié. Right arm opens. Body and head face side 3.

—Jump up from the right foot as the left leg passes through first position with a battement to second position in the air (45°), turning to the right with the back to the audience. Both arms meet in first position en avant. Look over the left shoulder toward side 3.

—Continue turning in the air to the right, coming down on the left foot in demi-plié facing front with the right foot sur le cou-de-pied front. Arms remain in first position en avant. Head spots to side 3.

Saut de basque

SAUT DE BASQUE—COUNT *and, three, four* (SLOW TEMPO):   Same as count *and, one, two.*

EMBOÎTÉS EN TOURNANT—COUNT *and, five* (FAST TEMPO):   Jump to the right from the left foot with a half-turn to the right so the back is to the audience. Bring the left foot sur le cou-de-pied front with the right leg in demi-plié. The right arm opens to second position as left arm moves forward to first position en avant. Look over the left shoulder to side 3.

Jump from the right foot with a half-turn to the right so that the body faces front again, coming down on the left foot in demi-plié with the right foot sur le cou-de-pied front. The left arm opens to second position as the right arm moves in to first position en avant. The head spots to side 3.

EMBOÎTÉS EN TOURNANT—COUNT *and, six* (FAST TEMPO):   Same as count *and, five.*

Assemblé dessous—count *and, seven* (fast tempo): Jump off the left foot and straighten the right leg to second position in the air (45°) toward side 3. Arms open slightly in low second position. Body and head face front.

—Come down closing the right leg back in fifth position demi-plié. Arms lower to preparatory position. Body and head face front.

Sous-sus sur les pointes—count *and, eight:* Relevé on both feet in fifth position sur les pointes with the left foot front. Arms rise through first position en avant to third position en haut rounded. Body and head face front. Body inclines slightly to the left.

SIX

This combination moves straight to side 7.

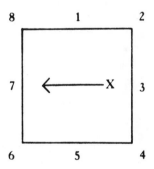

Saut de basque—count *and, one, two* (slow tempo): Arms open outward to second position with the left arm continuing to first position en avant with a coupé onto the right foot in demi-plié. The left foot rises to sur le cou-de-pied front in preparation for the jump. Continue as in combination five—count *and, one, two,* but to the opposite side.

Saut de basque—count *and, three, four* (slow tempo): Same as combination five—count *and, one, two,* but done to the opposite side.

EMBOÎTÉS EN TOURNANT—COUNT *and, five* (FAST TEMPO) : Same as combination FIVE—count *and, five,* but done to the opposite side.

EMBOÎTÉS EN TOURNANT—COUNT *and, six* (FAST TEMPO) : Same as combination FIVE—count *and, five,* but done to the opposite side.

ASSEMBLÉ DESSOUS—COUNT *and, seven* (FAST TEMPO) : Same as combination FIVE—count *and, seven,* but done to the opposite side.

SOUS-SUS SUR LES POINTES—COUNT *and, eight:* Same as combination FIVE—count *and, eight* but done to the opposite side.

SEVEN

This combination moves to the right toward side 3.
This series of turns should be done as smoothly as possible.

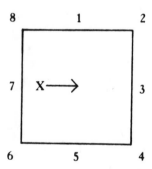

EMBOÎTÉS EN TOURNANT SUR LES POINTES—COUNT *and, one, two:* Demi-plié on the left foot and dégagé right foot front toward side 3 with the right arm front in first position, the left arm in second position. Look right to side 3.

—Piqué onto the right pointe, at the same time bringing the left foot retiré to front of the right knee, and make a half-turn to the right so that the back is to the audience. The right arm opens to second position as the left arm moves forward to first position en avant. Look over the left shoulder toward side 3.

Emboîtés en tournant

—Remain sur la pointe on the right foot and bring the left foot back of the right foot sur la pointe, at the same time making a half-turn to the right and raising the right foot retiré to the front of the left knee. The left arm opens to second position while the right arm moves forward to first position en avant. Body faces side 3. Head spots to side 3.

EMBOÎTÉS EN TOURNANT SUR LES POINTES—COUNT *and, three, four:* Same as count *and, one, two.*

EMBOÎTÉS EN TOURNANT SUR LES POINTES—COUNT *and, five, six:* Same as count *and, one, **two.***

EMBOÎTÉS EN TOURNANT SUR LES POINTES—COUNT *and, seven, eight:* Same as count *and, one, two.*

EIGHT

This combination continues moving to the right toward side 3.

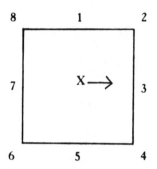

This combination finishes the series of turns begun in combination SEVEN.

FOUR CHAÎNÉS-DÉBOULÉS TOURS—COUNT *and one, and two, and three, and four:* With a demi-plié on the left leg, dégagé the right foot front effacé toward side 3 and piqué onto the right pointe, continuing with four chaîné-déboulé turns sur les pointes to side 3. The right arm opens and then both arms meet in first position en avant and remain there during the turns. Head spots to side 3.

SOUTENU EN TOURNANT—COUNT *and five, and six:* With a demi-plié on the left leg, dégagé the right foot front effacé toward side 3 and draw the left foot into fifth position front rising onto the pointes, pivoting on both feet to the right to face side 5, with the back to the audience. The right arm opens and then both arms meet in first position en avant. Look to the left over the left shoulder toward side 3.

—Pivot on both feet to the right and, remaining sur les pointes in fifth position, change the position of the feet so that the right foot finishes fifth position front sur les pointes facing the audience. After spotting to side 3, the head finishes facing front to the audience.

FOURTH POSITION—COUNT *and seven, and eight:* Remaining sur les pointes in a strong fifth position, raise the right foot retiré to the side of the left knee, while remaining sur la pointe on the left leg. Both arms rise to third position en haut from first position en avant. Body and head face audience.

With a small échappé, open the right foot back into fourth position croisé in plié à quart with the left leg in demi-plié and the right leg extended back with a straight knee and the foot flat on the floor. The right arm moves downward and forward with the palm facing downward in third arabesque position. The left arm opens outward to second position with the palm facing downward. Body faces corner 2. Look toward the right hand.

SILVER FAIRY
VARIATION

From the Ballet

The Sleeping Beauty

La Belle au Bois Dormant

SILVER FAIRY VARIATION

This is the second solo variation from the first Pas de Quatre in Act III of *The Sleeping Beauty* ballet. MUSIC by Peter Ilyich Tchaikovsky. CHOREOGRAPHY by Marius Petipa. As TAUGHT by Ludmilla Shollar and Anatole Vilzak. NOTATED by Laurencia Klaja. TEMPO 2/4, polka. Allegro giusto.

Recommended Recordings

1. *Tchaikovsky. Sleeping Beauty Highlights.* London Symphony Orchestra, conducted by Pierre Monteux. London Records, London FFRR, Stereo Treasury Series, STS 15179. Side 2: The Silver Fairy variation is the fifth selection.

2. *The Sleeping Beauty Ballet. Complete.* Richard Bonynge, conductor, with the National Philharmonic Orchestra. London Records, London FFRR, CSA 2316. Side 5: Act III. This variation follows the Gold Fairy variation.

Piano Music

Complete Piano Music for The Sleeping Beauty Ballet, by Peter Ilyich Tchaikovsky. Variation II, Polka, The Silver Fairy, page 164. Published by The Tschaikovsky Foundation, 1950.

Comments

The Silver Fairy's variation to the tune of a lively polka in Act III of *The Sleeping Beauty* ballet celebrates the wedding of Princess Aurora to Prince Florimund (sometimes called Prince Désiré or Prince Charming). The Silver Fairy variation has survived in both the Pas de Quatre and Pas de Trois versions of the choreography and is one of the most well known and well preserved variations of Petipa. In the Pas de Trois version of Florestan and his two sisters, the choreography of the Silver Fairy is danced by one of the sisters and the Diamond Fairy choreography is danced by the other sister.

According to the *Borzoi Book of Ballets,** the Silver Fairy was included as the fifth variation in the ballet *Princess Aurora,* a one-act version of *The Sleeping Beauty* ballet, and was described as follows:

"The fifth variation is one of the gayest in the whole of classical ballet as we know it. It includes very fast passés on pointe, each passé gaining height. From an entrechat-trois, she steps into an arabesque. She hops on pointe with tiny steps, finishing with a relevé into attitude en avant."

* *Grace Robert,* Borzoi Book of Ballets *(New York: Alfred A. Knopf, 1946). Now out of print.*

INTRODUCTION

Stand at center stage.

COUNT *one* THROUGH *six* (SLOWLY): Stand with the right leg pointe tendue back croisé on the floor with the knee relaxed. Arms are in low second position. Body faces corner 2. Look toward the audience.

ONE

This combination moves to the right on a diagonal toward corner 2, then toward corner 6.

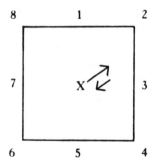

PIQUÉ DE COTÉ—COUNT *and, one:* Demi-plié on the left leg with a dégagé of the right leg to the side raised slightly off the floor. Step sideways toward corner 2 onto the right pointe, bringing the left foot retiré to the front of the right knee. The right arm moves gracefully to the front of the chest with the palm facing toward the body. The elbow is bent and raised a little way from the body; left arm is in second position. Body faces front to audience; look right toward corner 2.

PIQUÉ DE COTÉ—COUNT *two:* Same as count *one.*

JETÉ DESSUS—COUNT *and:* Come down in demi-plié on the left foot with the right foot sur le cou-de-pied back. Quickly execute a small jeté to the side with the right leg finishing in demi-plié front in the spot vacated by the left foot, bringing the left foot sur le cou-de-pied back. The right arm opens straight outward and downward by straightening the elbow with the palm facing upward; the left arm remains in second position. Body faces audience and inclines to the right. Look toward the right hand in the direction of corner 2.

PIQUÉ EN ARRIÈRE CLOSING FIFTH POSITION SUR LES POINTES—COUNT *three:* Immediately step backward onto the left pointe toward corner 6, bringing the right foot retiré to the front of the left knee, quickly closing the right foot front croisé to fifth position sur les pointes. The left arm moves gracefully to the front of the chest with the palm facing the body with the elbow bent and raised away from the body slightly; the right arm moves to second position. Body faces audience; look toward corner 8.

TWO

This combination moves to the left on a diagonal toward corner 8, then toward corner 4.

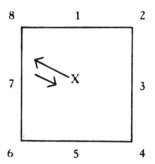

Repeat combination ONE to the opposite side. Instead of finishing fifth position sur les pointes, finish in fifth position demi-plié with left foot front en face at center stage on count *three*.

THREE

*This combination moves backward toward side 5
in a very quick tempo with accent down.*

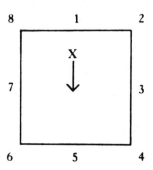

RELEVÉ PASSÉ EN ARRIÈRE WITH LEFT FOOT—COUNT *and:* From fifth position demi-plié with the left foot front, spring onto the right pointe, at the same time raising the left foot retiré to the side of right knee. Then close the left foot back fifth position demi-plié en face, accent down. The left arm opens outward through first position en avant to a wide first position, opening the palm toward the audience, while the right arm remains in second position. (Arms may also move gradually upward from preparatory position through first position en avant to third position en haut during the seven counts of music.) Body faces audience; look toward left palm as it moves outward.

RELEVÉ PASSÉ EN ARRIÈRE WITH RIGHT FOOT—COUNT *one:* Same as count *and,* but done to the opposite side.

RELEVÉ PASSÉ EN ARRIÈRE WITH LEFT FOOT—COUNT *two:* Same as count *and.*

RELEVÉ PASSÉ EN ARRIÈRE WITH RIGHT FOOT—COUNT *three:* Same as count *and,* but done to the opposite side.

RELEVÉ PASSÉ EN ARRIÈRE WITH LEFT FOOT—COUNT *four:* Same as count *and.*

RELEVÉ PASSÉ EN ARRIÈRE WITH RIGHT FOOT—COUNT *five:* Same as count *and,* but done to the opposite side.

RELEVÉ PASSÉ EN ARRIÈRE WITH LEFT FOOT—COUNT *six:* Same as count *and.*

RELEVÉ PASSÉ EN ARRIÈRE WITH RIGHT FOOT FINISHING SUR LE COU-DE-PIED BACK—COUNT *and, seven:* Same as count *and,* but done to the opposite side. Instead of finishing fifth position back with the right foot, come down on the left foot in fondu (demi-plié) and bring the right foot sur le cou-de-pied back. (If arms are in third position en haut, open them to second position.)

FOUR

Repeat combination ONE exactly.

FIVE

Repeat combination TWO exactly.

SIX

This combination moves backward toward side 5.

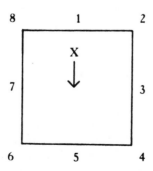

Repeat combination THREE through count *six.* Continue as follows:

RELEVÉ DEVANT WITH RIGHT FOOT—COUNT *and:* From fifth position demi-plié with the right foot front, spring onto the left pointe, at the same time raising the right foot retiré in front of the left knee. The right arm opens outward to second position as the left arm remains in second position. Body and head face audience.

FIFTH POSITION DEMI-PLIÉ WITH RIGHT FOOT FRONT—COUNT *seven:* Close the right foot front in fifth position demi-plié. Both arms move downward to preparatory position. Body and head face front; look downward.

SEVEN

This combination begins at center stage, moves toward side 3, and then changes direction to face corner 8.

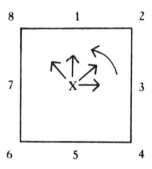

STEP-GLISSÉ EN AVANT, RELEVÉ ARABESQUE—COUNT *and, one:* Slide forward quickly onto the right foot toward side 3 into a demi-plié with weight forward. With a slight spring, relevé onto the right pointe, raising the left leg back in arabesque effacée. Both arms open outward through second position to third position en haut on the glissade. On the relevé arabesque, both arms move downward through first position en avant and then open into first arabesque position with right arm front, with a sweeping movement. Body and head face side 3.

EMBOÎTÉ FRONT WITH RIGHT FOOT—COUNT *and:* From arabesque position fall back onto the left foot into fondu (demi-plié) and, with a slight spring, raise the right foot front effacé in the air with the knee slightly bent. Both arms open to second position. Body and head face side 3.

EMBOÎTÉ FRONT WITH LEFT FOOT—COUNT *two:* With a slight spring on the left foot, jump into the air bringing the left foot front croisé with knee bent. Come down on the right foot in demi-plié, at the same time changing the direction of the body to face corner 2. Arms begin to move upward through second position. Body faces croisé to corner 2. Look toward corner 2.

EMBOÎTÉ FRONT WITH RIGHT FOOT—COUNT *and:* With a slight spring on the right foot, jump into the air bringing the right foot front with knee bent. Come down on the left foot in demi-plié, at the same time changing the direction of the body to face front. Arms are moving upward toward third position en haut rounded. Body and head face front en face to audience.

EMBOÎTÉ FRONT WITH LEFT FOOT—COUNT *three:* With a slight spring on the left foot, jump into the air bringing the left foot front effacé with knee bent. Come down on the right foot in demi-plié, at the same time changing the direction of the body to face corner 8. Arms have now reached third position en haut rounded. Body faces effacé to corner 8; look toward the arms.

EIGHT

Repeat combination SEVEN to the opposite side.

NINE

Repeat combination SEVEN exactly.

TEN

---

*This combination begins at center stage, moves toward side 7,
and then changes direction to face corner 8.*

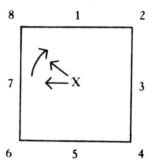

Repeat combination SEVEN, count *and one, and two* to the opposite
side. Continue as follows.

ASSEMBLÉ COUPÉ DEVANT—COUNT *and:*   From demi-plié on the left
foot with right foot front in the air croisé with knee bent, spring
off the left foot, and, without brushing out, close the right foot
front fifth position croisé. Arms are in preparatory position. Body
and head face corner 8.

SOUS-SUS SUR LES POINTES—COUNT *three:*   Relevé into fifth position sur les pointes with the knees bent. Arms pass through first
position en avant to third position en haut. Body faces croisé to
corner 8. Look toward audience.

ELEVEN

This combination remains in place at center stage.

*Two sautés in fifth position
sur les pointes*

TWO SAUTÉS IN FIFTH POSITION SUR LES POINTES—COUNT *and:* Remaining on the pointes in fifth position croisé with knees bent, hop quickly twice on the pointes. Arms are in third position en haut rounded. Body faces croisé to corner 8. Look right toward the audience.

TOMBÉ DESSOUS RAISE RIGHT FOOT FRONT—COUNT *one:* Come down in fondu (demi-plié) on the left foot, at the same time bringing the right foot front croisé sur le cou-de-pied. Arms open quickly outward to second position from third position en haut with palms facing upward. Body faces croisé to corner 8. Head inclines to the right while looking front to audience.

TEMPS LEVÉ, RAISE LEFT FOOT BACK—COUNT *two:* Spring up off the left foot and come down on the right foot with the left foot sur le cou-de-pied back. Arms close downward to preparatory position. Body remains facing croisé to corner 8. Head turns slightly to the left toward corner 8; look downward.

TEMPS LEVÉ, RAISE RIGHT FOOT FRONT—COUNT *and:* Spring up off the right foot and come down on the left foot in demi-plié with the right foot front croisé sur le cou-de-pied. Arms remain in preparatory position. Body remains facing croisé to corner 8. Head straightens; look front toward audience.

ASSEMBLÉ COUPÉ DESSOUS—COUNT *three:* Spring up off the left foot and close the right foot fifth position back demi-plié (without brushing the leg out), changing épaulement so that body faces corner 2 with the left foot front croisé. Arms remain in preparatory position. Body faces corner 2. Head turns slightly to the right toward corner 2; look downward.

TWELVE

This combination remains in place at center stage.

SOUS-SUS WITH TWO SAUTÉS SUR LES POINTES IN FIFTH POSITION—COUNT *and:* Relevé into fifth position sur les pointes with the left foot front and the knees bent. Immediately hop quickly twice on the pointes. Arms rise to third position en haut rounded. Body faces croisé to corner 2. Look left toward the audience.

TOMBÉ DESSOUS RAISE LEFT FOOT FRONT—COUNT *one:* Same as combination ELEVEN—count *one,* but done to the opposite side.

TEMPS LEVÉ, RAISE RIGHT FOOT BACK—COUNT *two:*   Same as combination ELEVEN—count *two,* but done to the opposite side.

TEMPS LEVÉ, RAISE LEFT FOOT FRONT; ASSEMBLÉ COUPÉ DESSOUS—COUNT *and, three:*   Same as combination ELEVEN—count *and, three,* but done to the opposite side.

THIRTEEN

Repeat combination TWELVE to the opposite side,
except that count *and, three* becomes count *three, four.*

FOURTEEN

This combination remains in place at center stage.

This combination is a continuation of combination THIRTEEN.

TWO SAUTÉS IN FIFTH POSITION SUR LES POINTES; TOMBÉ DESSOUS, RAISE LEFT FOOT FRONT—COUNT *five:*   Same as combination ELEVEN—count *and, one,* but done to the opposite side.

TEMPS LEVÉ, RAISE RIGHT FOOT BACK—COUNT *six:*   Same as combination ELEVEN—count *two,* but done to the opposite side.

ASSEMBLÉ COUPÉ DERRIÈRE—COUNT *seven:*   Spring up off the left foot with the right foot sur le cou-de-pied back and come down in fifth position demi-plié with right foot back. Arms are in preparatory position. Body faces corner 2. Head is turned slightly to the right toward corner 2; look downward.

FIFTEEN†

This combination moves toward side 3.

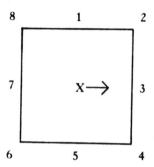

DRAW RIGHT POINTE BACK ALONG FLOOR—COUNT *and:* Turn body to face side 7, at the same time moving right foot effacé back with knee bent and the pointe of the right foot resting on the floor; the left leg is in demi-plié. Keeping the right pointe on the floor, first draw the flat of the left foot toward the right foot moving backward toward side 3. At the same time straighten the left knee while keeping the right leg bent. Then demi-plié on the left foot as soon as it reaches the right foot, releasing the right pointe from the floor so that it is sur le cou-de-pied back, ready to repeat the movement. Arms are in low second position with hands at edge of tutu skirt. Body faces side 7; look toward corner 2.

DRAW RIGHT POINTE BACK ALONG FLOOR—COUNT *one:* Continue stepping backward toward side 3. Keep the right pointe on the floor with the right knee bent in effacé position and draw the flat of the left foot toward the right foot. Arms remain in low second position with hands at edge of tutu skirt. Body remains facing side 7; remain looking toward corner 2.

DRAW RIGHT POINTE BACK ALONG FLOOR—COUNT *two:* Same as count *one.*

† *For an alternate version, see notes at the end of this variation.*

PIQUÉ ARABESQUE ON RIGHT LEG—COUNT *and:* In demi-plié on the left leg, with right foot sur le cou-de-pied back, change direction of body to face right to side 3, and piqué on the right foot to side 3, lifting the left leg back into arabesque effacée. Both arms extend forward to side 3 with the right arm slightly higher. Elbows are straight. Palms face downward. Body and head face side 3.

CLOSE FIFTH POSITION SUR LES POINTES—COUNT *three:* Remaining on the right pointe, close the left leg back in fifth position effacé sur les pointes. Arms move downward to low second position with hands on the edge of tutu. Body and head face side 3.

SIXTEEN

This combination moves toward side 7.

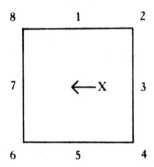

Repeat combination FIFTEEN to the opposite side.

SEVENTEEN

This combination moves toward side 3 and then moves diagonally toward corner 2.

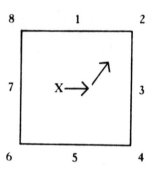

DRAW RIGHT POINTE BACK ALONG FLOOR FOUR TIMES—COUNT *and, one, two, three:* Same as combination FIFTEEN—count *and, one, two,* but repeat one more time.

PIQUÉ ARABESQUE ON RIGHT LEG—COUNT *four:* In demi-plié on the left leg, bring right foot sur le cou-de-pied back, change direction of body to face right, and piqué on the right foot to side 3, lifting the left leg back into arabesque effacée. Arms move to first arabesque position with the right arm front. Body and head face side 3.

CLOSE FIFTH POSITION SUR LES POINTES—COUNT *five:* Remaining sur la pointe on the right leg, bring the left foot to front croisé fifth position sur les pointes. Arms move downward to low second position. Body and head face corner 2.

EMBOÎTÉ SUR LES POINTES WITH RIGHT LEG—COUNT *six:* Remaining sur la pointe on the left foot, open the right foot to the side slightly off the floor moving forward to corner 2. Close the right foot fifth position front sur les pointes effacé. Arms are in low second position. Body and head face corner 2; look downward.

EMBOÎTÉ SUR LES POINTES WITH LEFT LEG AND CLOSE IN DEMI-PLIÉ
IN FIFTH POSITION—COUNT *and:* Same as count *six,* but done
to the opposite side. Immediately demi-plié in fifth position croisé
with the left foot front. Arms lower to preparatory position. Body
and head face corner 2.

Relevé attitude front croisé

RELEVÉ ATTITUDE FRONT CROISÉ (FINAL POSE)—COUNT
seven: From fifth position demi-plié, spring up in relevé onto
the right pointe, at the same time raising the left leg attitude
front croisé. Hold this pose for a moment. Both arms pass
through first position as right arm continues to third position en
haut and left arm opens to second position. Body faces corner 2;
look left toward the audience.

Notes

The following is a more commonly danced version of the last part of this variation.

FIFTEEN

This combination remains in place at center stage.

ENTRECHAT-TROIS DERRIÈRE EFFACÉ—COUNT *and, one:* From demi-plié in fifth position with the left foot front, jump up off both feet and beat the calves together. Come down on the right foot in demi-plié, at the same time bringing the left foot sur le cou-de-pied back croisé. Arms are in low second position. Body and head face corner 8.

PIQUÉ ARABESQUE—COUNT *two:* Change direction of the body to face left to side 7 and piqué on the left foot to side 7, lifting the right leg back into arabesque effacée. Arms are in first arabesque position with the left arm extended front. Body and head face side 7.

CLOSE INTO FIFTH POSITION DEMI-PLIÉ—COUNT *and, three:* Close the right leg front in fifth position croisé. Arms move downward to low second position. Body and head face corner 8.

SIXTEEN

Repeat combination FIFTEEN to the opposite side.

SEVENTEEN

This combination remains in place at center stage and then moves diagonally toward corner 2.

Entrechat-trois derrière effacé—count *and:* Same as combination FIFTEEN—count *and, one.*

Piqué arabesqe—count *one:* Same as combination FIFTEEN—count *two.*

Close into fifth position demi-plié—count *two:* Same as combination FIFTEEN—count *and, three.*

Entrechat-trois derrière effacé—count *three:* Same as combination FIFTEEN—count *and, one,* but done to the opposite side.

Piqué arabesque—count *four:* Same as combination FIFTEEN—count *two,* but done to the opposite side.

Close fifth position sur les pointes—count *five:* Remaining sur la pointe on right leg, bring the left foot to front croisé fifth position sur les pointes. Arms moves downward to low second position. Body and head face corner 2.

Emboîté sur les pointes with right leg—count *six:* Remaining sur la pointe on the left foot, open the right foot to the side slightly off the floor, moving forward to corner 2. Close the right foot fifth position front sur les pointes effacé. Arms are in low second position. Body and head face corner 2. Look downward.

Emboîté sur les pointes with left leg, close in fifth position demi-plié—count *and:* Same as count *six,* done to the opposite side, but immediately demi-plié in fifth position croisé with left foot front. Arms lower to preparatory position. Body and head face corner 2.

Relevé attitude front croisé (final pose)—count *seven:* From fifth position demi-plié, spring up in relevé onto the right pointe, at the same time raising the left leg attitude front croisé. Hold the pose for a moment. Both arms pass through first position as right arm continues to third position en haut and the left arm opens to second position. Body faces corner 2; look left toward the audience.

DIAMOND FAIRY
VARIATION

From the Ballet

La Belle au Bois Dormant

DIAMOND FAIRY VARIATION

This is the fourth solo variation from the first Pas de Quatre in Act III of *The Sleeping Beauty* ballet. MUSIC by Peter Ilyich Tchaikovsky. CHOREOGRAPHY by Marius Petipa. As TAUGHT by Ludmilla Shollar and Anatole Vilzak. NOTATED by Laurencia Klaja. TEMPO 2/4, vivace.

Recommended Recordings

1. *Tchaikovsky. Sleeping Beauty Highlights.* London Symphony Orchestra, conducted by Pierre Monteux. London Records, London FFRR, Stereo Treasury Series, STS 15179. Side 2: The Diamond Fairy variation is the sixth selection and follows the Silver Fairy variation.

2. *The Sleeping Beauty Ballet. Complete.* Richard Bonynge, conductor, with the National Philharmonic Orchestra. London Records, London FFRR, CSA 2316. Side 5: Act III. This is the last variation before the Coda. It follows the Sapphire Fairy variation.

Piano Music

Complete Piano Music for *The Sleeping Beauty Ballet,* by Peter Ilyich Tchaikovsky. Variation IV, Diamond, page 167. Published by The Tschaikovsky Foundation, 1950.

Comments

The Diamond variation is the fourth and last variation of this Pas de Quatre from Act III of *The Sleeping Beauty* ballet that is notated here. (Variation III, Sapphire, is omitted because it was never taught in the variation classes of Madame Shollar, Anatole Vilzak, or Barbara Fallis and is so seldom performed on the stage that the original choreography seems to have been completely lost. Using the music of the Sapphire variation, Rudolf Nureyev added a male variation to the Pas de Quatre making it a Pas de Cinq in his production.)

The tempo is brilliantly quick and is introduced by the tiny bell-like tones of the triangle. The choreography consists of many quick, small jumps interspersed with steps on pointe, and ends with a pas de chat.

This variation is an exercise in quick timing and is in contrast to the terre à terre choreography of most of the other variations in the ballet.

INTRODUCTION

Stand at center stage facing audience.

COUNT *one* THROUGH *six* (VERY LIGHTLY AND QUICKLY): Stand in fourth position with left leg front in demi-plié and right leg back, with knee straight and foot flat on the floor. Arms are in wide first position front with palms facing downward. Alternating right and left, flick the wrists with an upward movement of the palm, keeping the shoulders stationary and elbows relaxed.

Count *one:* Flick right wrist.

Count *two:*   Flick left wrist.
Count *three:*   Flick right wrist.
Count *four:*   Flick left wrist.
Count *five:*   Flick right wrist.
Count *six:*   Flick left wrist.

ONE

This combination moves quickly toward side 3 and then toward side 7.

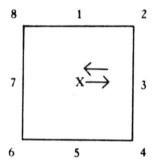

PAS DE BOURRÉE COURU EN PREMIÈRE SUR LES POINTES—COUNT *and:*   Quickly dégagé right foot toward side 3 and run in first position sur les pointes with two quick, tiny steps toward side 3, right foot, left foot. Arms are in low second position. Body and head face corner 2.

POINTE TENDUE TO SECOND POSITION À TERRE—COUNT *one:*   Demi-plié on left foot and pointe tendue right foot to the side on the floor toward side 3. The right arm is in first position en avant and left arm is in second position. Body and head incline to right toward the right leg.

PAS DE BOURRÉE CHANGÉE DESSOUS—COUNT *and:*   With a strong, quick push of the right leg, draw the right leg behind the left leg sur les demi-pointes. Open the left leg to second position on the floor, remaining on the demi-pointes, and quickly demi-plié on the left foot, bringing the right foot dégagé front croisé toward corner 8. Arms are in low second position. Body first faces front and then changes to face corner 8.

PIQUÉ EN AVANT CROISÉ—COUNT *two:* Piqué forward onto the right pointe toward corner 8, bringing the left foot retiré back of the right knee. Bring both arms forward and cross them over the chest with the right hand on top; palms are gracefully curved and face toward the body. Body bends slightly back and faces corner 8. Look toward audience over right shoulder.

TWO

This combination quickly moves left toward side 7 and then to the right toward side 3.

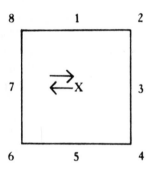

This combination continues combination ONE.

PAS DE BOURRÉE COURU EN PREMIÈRE SUR LES POINTES; POINTE TENDUE TO SECOND POSITION À TERRE—COUNT *and, three:* Demi-plié on the right leg with left foot sur le cou-de-pied back and repeat count *and, one* to the opposite side.

PAS DE BOURRÉE CHANGÉE DESSOUS; PIQUÉ EN AVANT CROISÉ— COUNT *and, four:* Same as count *and, two,* but done to the opposite side.

THREE

This combination remains in place at center stage.

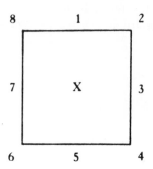

This combination continues combination TWO.

ENTRECHAT-TROIS—COUNT *and:*   Close right foot back into fifth position demi-plié en face and jump into the air off both feet, beating the left leg in front of the right leg. Come down on the right foot in demi-plié with the left foot sur le cou-de-pied back. The left arm is in first position en avant; right arm is in second position. Body and head incline slightly to the left side facing front.

ASSEMBLÉ COUPÉ DERRIÈRE—COUNT *five:*   Jump into the air off the right foot with the left foot sur le cou-de-pied back and come down in fifth position demi-plié en face, closing the left foot back without brushing the leg out. Arms move to low second position. Body and head straighten en face.

ENTRECHAT-TROIS; ASSEMBLÉ COUPÉ DERRIÈRE—COUNT *and, six:* Same as count *and, five,* but done to the opposite side.

ENTRECHAT-TROIS; ASSEMBLÉ COUPÉ DERRIÈRE—COUNT *and, seven:* Same as count *and, five.*

ENTRECHAT-TROIS; ASSEMBLÉ COUPÉ DERRIÈRE—COUNT *and, eight:* Same as count *and, five,* but done to the opposite side.

Assemblé coupé derrière

FOUR

Repeat combination ONE exactly.

FIVE

Repeat combination TWO exactly.

SIX

Repeat combination THREE exactly.

SEVEN

This combination moves diagonally back upstage toward corner 6.

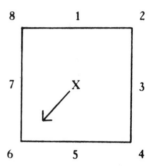

TEMPS LEVÉ WITH DÉVELOPPÉ À LA SECONDE—COUNT *one:* Jump up on the left foot and at the same time open the right leg to second position in the air (45°) with a développé. Remain in place facing front. Arms open to second position; body and head face front. (Can also be done with pointe tendue à terre with right leg.)

JETÉ DESSOUS—COUNT *two:* Remaining in the same spot, temps levé on the left leg with the right leg in second position in the air and come down on the right foot, in the spot vacated by the left foot, as the left foot rises front sur le cou-de-pied. Left arm moves to first position en avant; right arm is in second position. Body and head remain facing front.

SAUT DE BASQUE—COUNT *three, four:* Step to the left side on the left foot, thrust the right leg into the air in second position, turning the back to the audience to face corner 6, and jump up off the left foot. Arms open to low second position. Head looks over the right shoulder toward corner 6.

—Come down facing front in demi-plié on the right foot, with the left foot sur le cou-de-pied front. Left arm passes through preparatory position to first position en avant as right arm opens to second position from first position. Body and head face front.

TEMPS LEVÉ WITH DÉVELOPPÉ À LA SECONDE—COUNT *five:* Same as count *one,* beginning with a tombé onto left foot front with right foot sur le cou-de-pied back.

JETÉ DESSOUS—COUNT *six:* Same as count *two.*

SAUT DE BASQUE—COUNT *seven, eight:* Same as count *three, four.*

EIGHT

This combination retraces the diagonal from corner 6 toward corner 2. The tempo becomes faster.

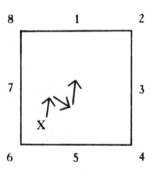

GLISSADE DEVANT—COUNT *one:* Facing downstage corner 2, execute a glissade to the left without changing the feet, finishing with the left foot fifth position front demi-plié. Both arms open to low second position. Body and head face corner 2.

Jeté dessous

JETÉ DESSOUS—COUNT *two:* Brush left foot to the side in low second position in the air, at the same time jumping up off the right
foot. Come down on the left foot slightly in front of the spot vacated by the right foot, at the same time bringing the right foot
sur le cou-de-pied front. The left arm moves upward to third position en haut passing directly through second position; right arm
is in second position. (Each arm alternates moving back and forth
from second to third position, without passing through first position, on each of the following jetés.) Body and head incline to
the left.

GLISSADE DEVANT—COUNT *three:* Same as count *one,* but done to
the opposite side.

JETÉ DESSOUS—COUNT *four:* Same as count *two,* but done to the
opposite side.

GLISSADE DEVANT—COUNT *five:*   Same as count *one.*

JETÉ DESSOUS—COUNT *six:*   Same as count *two.*

GLISSADE DEVANT—COUNT *seven:*   Same as count *one,* but done to the opposite side.

ASSEMBLÉ DESSOUS—COUNT *eight:*   Jump up on the left foot, at the same time executing a battement to second position in the air with the right leg. Close the right leg fifth position back croisé in demi-plié. The left arm opens outward to second position; right arm is already in second position. Body straightens as body and head face croisé to corner 2.

NINE

Repeat combination SEVEN exactly.

TEN

This combination retraces the diagonal from corner 6 toward corner 2.

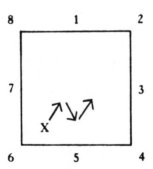

Repeat combination EIGHT up through count *six:* (Omit count seven.) Continue as follows:

ASSEMBLÉ DESSOUS—COUNT *seven:* Same as combination EIGHT—count *eight.*

SOUS-SUS SUR LES POINTES—COUNT *eight:* From fifth position demi-plié, spring up into a relevé to fifth position sur les pointes in place with left foot front. The left arm passes through first position en avant to third position en haut; right arm is in second position. Body and head face front.

ELEVEN

This combination moves to the left toward side 7.

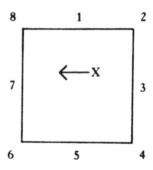

PAS DE BOURRÉE EN CINQUIÈME SUR PLACE—COUNT *and:* Remaining in fifth position sur les pointes, execute two tiny steps in fifth position sur les pointes in place, accenting the foot that is front, left foot, right foot. The left arm remains in third position en haut rounded; right arm remains in second position. Body and head face front.

RETIRÉ EN AVANT—COUNT *one:* Remaining sur la pointe on the right foot, and bending the right knee slightly, raise the left leg retiré to the front of the right knee. Arms remain the same. Body inclines slightly forward from the waist. Head inclines forward and straightens with a nodding movement; look downward.

PAS DE BOURRÉE EN CINQUIÈME SUR PLACE; RETIRÉ EN AVANT—COUNT *and, two:* Same as count *and, one.*

PAS DE BOURRÉE EN CINQUIÈME SUR PLACE; RETIRÉ EN AVANT—COUNT *and, three:* Same as count *and, one.*

TOMBÉ EN AVANT—COUNT *and:* Fall forward onto the left foot into demi-plié at the same time raising the right foot to sur le cou-de-pied back. The left arm moves directly downward to first position en avant; right arm remains in second position. Body inclines to the left; look over left arm to side 7.

BALLONNÉ À LA SECONDE—COUNT *four:* Step onto the right foot into demi-plié behind the left foot. Raise the left leg to second position in the air, without développé, at the same time jumping up off the right foot. Come down in demi-plié on the right foot, at the same time bending the left knee and bringing the left foot sur le cou-de-pied front. The left arm remains in first position en avant; right arm remains in second position. Body faces front and inclines to the left; look over the left arm.

SAUT DE BASQUE—COUNT *and, five:* Without glissade, step to the left side in demi-plié on the left foot and thrust the right leg into second position in the air, at the same time turning the back to the audience and jumping off the left foot. Arms are in low second position. Body faces back. Look over right shoulder toward side 7.

—Continue turning to the left in the air. Come down facing front on the right foot in demi-plié with the left foot sur le cou-de-pied front. Arms meet in first position en avant during the turn in the air and finish with the left arm first position en avant and the right arm in second position. Body and head face front.

SAUT DE BASQUE—COUNT *and, six:* Same as count *and, five.*

SAUT DE BASQUE—COUNT *and, seven:* Same as count *and, five.*

ASSEMBLÉ DESSOUS—COUNT *and:* Jump up off the right leg, at the
same time straightening the left knee to second position in the
air. Close the left leg to fifth position back demi-plié. Arms open
slightly to low second position. Body and head face front.

SOUS-SUS SUR LES POINTES—COUNT *eight:* Relevé into fifth position sur les pointes with the right foot front. The right arm passes
through first position en avant to third position en haut rounded;
left arm is in second position. Body and head face front.

TWELVE

*This combination moves to the right toward side 3,
and then diagonally to corner 2.*

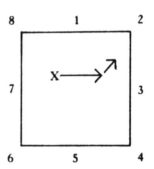

Repeat combination ELEVEN through count *and, seven* to the opposite
side. Continue as follows.

STEP RIGHT FOOT, STEP LEFT FOOT—COUNT *and:* Step to the right
(side 3) on the right foot; then step over the right foot with the
left foot into demi-plié (on both feet) fourth position croisé. Arms
are in low second position. Body faces corner 2; look toward
corner 2.

PAS DE CHAT, POINTE TENDUE CROISÉE BACK—COUNT *eight:* Jump
up off the left foot, at the same time raising and bending the
right knee, and travel diagonally to the right toward corner 2.
As the right foot begins to descend, raise and bend left knee and
land first on the right foot in demi-plié and then on the left foot
front in fourth position croisé. Immediately straighten the left
knee and pointe tendue right foot back croisé with knee straight.
On the pas de chat, both arms move through first position en
avant upward to third position en haut. Then arms open outward, the right arm moving to first position en avant rounded,
the left arm moving to second position. On the pointe tendue
croisée back, the right arm extends forward with elbow straight,
palm facing upward. Body faces corner 2; look toward the audience.

SWAN QUEEN'S ACT II VARIATION

From the Ballet

Swan Lake

Le Lac des Cygnes

Cynthia Gregory

as the Swan Queen Odette in SWAN LAKE.

Alexandra Danilova

as the Swan Queen Odette in SWAN LAKE.

———————————————————

SWAN QUEEN'S
ACT II VARIATION

Prima ballerina variation from Act II of *The Swan Lake* (Le Lac des Cygnes) ballet. MUSIC by Peter Ilyich Tchaikovsky. CHOREOGRAPHY after Lev Ivanov. AS TAUGHT by Ludmilla Shollar, Anatole Vilzak, and Barbara Fallis. NOTATED AND ADAPTED by Laurencia Klaja. TEMPO 6/8, moderato assai.

Recommended Recording

Swan Lake Ballet Suite. New York Philharmonic, conducted by Leonard Bernstein. Columbia Records/CBS, Columbia Masterworks, STEREO M-30056. Side 1 : The Swan Queen's Variation in Act II is the third selection between a waltz and the music for the famous Pas de Quatre which is danced by the four little swans.

Piano Music

Le Lac des Cygnes (*The Swan Lake*) (*Lebedinoe Ozero* is the Russian title), by Peter Ilyich Tchaikovsky. Opus 20, Grand Ballet in Four Acts. Act II, No. 16, Swan Queen's variation, p. 82. Published by The Tschaikovsky Foundation, 1950.

Comments

The choreography of any ballet changes subtly, or not so subtly, as time goes by. Therefore, there are many versions of the ballet *Swan Lake* based on the choreography of Marius Petipa and Lev Ivanov. The choreography presented here is a composite version that follows the general outline of the original choreography done by Lev Ivanov, who choreographed Acts II and IV (the "white" acts).

The double role of Odette-Odile is a challenge to all ballerinas. Margot Fonteyn regarded it as the most difficult ballet in her repertoire. Sometimes Act II is given by itself, as in George Balanchine's version. At one time the Leningrad Kirov Ballet used one ballerina to play the part of Odette (the Swan Queen) and another ballerina to play the part of Odile (the Black Swan) during the same performance. During the Leningrad Kirov's appearances in New York, before her defection to the West, Natalia Makarova danced the role of Odette and Kaleria Fedicheva danced the role of Odile.

For the moment we will concentrate on the Swan Queen Odette's variation of Act II. The Swan Queen is an elusive, gentle, lyrical creature, in contrast to the arrogant, seductive Black Swan.

The back, head, arms, and hands play an important part in portraying the swanlike character of this role. Therefore, the choreography attempts to evoke birdlike images through certain preening and flying movements.

INTRODUCTION

Stand toward the back of center stage, facing the audience.

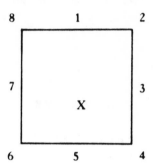

STAND WITH RIGHT LEG POINTE TENDUE BACK CROISÉ with knee bent (knees are together). Arms are in front of the body en bas with the left wrist crossed over the right wrist. Head is turned and inclined toward the left shoulder. Body is inclined slightly to the left.

COUNT *one, two:* Temps lié by transferring the weight of the body back onto the right foot and, with a passing movement through fourth position demi-plié, pointe tendue left foot front croisé with knees straight. Arms open to second position, with elbows relaxing and straightening like the wings of a bird. Head turns toward corner 2.

COUNT *three, four:* Transfer the weight of the body forward onto the left foot in demi-plié fourth position, with right leg extended back with straight knee and foot flat on the floor. Arms close front en bas with left wrist crossed over the right wrist. Head turns and inclines toward left shoulder. Body inclines to the left.

ONE

This combination moves forward toward the audience.

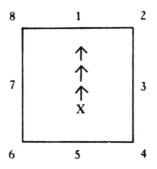

RELEVÉ ROND DE JAMBE EN L'AIR EN DEDANS—COUNT *and,*
   one: Relevé onto the left pointe, at the same time raising the
   right leg to second position (90°). Execute a single or double
   rond de jambe inward with the arms opening to second position.
   Head and body face écarté to corner 2.

—Remaining sur la pointe on the left leg, open the right leg higher
   than 90° in second position écarté, while turning the body
   slightly to the left toward corner 8. The right arm moves higher
   allongé in second position with a relaxing and straightening
   movement of the elbow. Head tilts slightly upward; look toward
   the right arm.

FOURTH POSITION—COUNT *and, two:* Bring right leg down through
   first position demi-plié and slide it forward to fourth position
   croisé demi-plié (plié à quart), with left leg back with straight
   knee, foot flat on the floor. Both arms move downward to front of
   body en bas so that the right wrist is crossed over the left wrist,
   with the palms curved inward. Head inclines and turns toward
   the right shoulder. Body inclines right.

RELEVÉ ROND DE JAMBE EN L'AIR EN DEDANS—COUNT *and,*
   three: Same as count *and, one,* but done to the opposite side.

Fourth position

Fourth position—count *four* (sustained): Same as count *and, two,* but done to the opposite side.

Relevé double rond de jambe en l'air en face—count *and, five:* Transfer weight of the body forward onto the left foot and relevé onto the left pointe, at the same time raising the right leg to second position in the air (90°) with the body facing front. Execute a double rond de jambe in the air. Head and body face front. Arms are in second position.

—Open the right leg to second position, remaining en face facing front. Both arms rise slightly higher in second position with the flying movement. Look toward corner 2.

Fifth position sur les pointes—count *and, six:* Hold balance in second position en l'air.

—Remaining sur la pointe on the left foot, close the right foot front fifth position sur les pointes. Arms remain in second position. Body and head are facing front.

PAS DE BOURRÉE CHANGÉE SUR LES POINTES—COUNT *and, seven:* Remaining sur les pointes, do a quick, tiny pas de bourrée changée in place: first cross the left pointe in front of the right pointe with the weight forward, then transfer the weight back to the right pointe and take a tiny step on the left pointe to the left side and cross the right pointe to front in fifth position with the weight forward. The accent is on the foot that is in front; that is, the accent is first on the left pointe and then on the right pointe. Arms are extended slightly back of the shoulder line in second position with the palms downward. Head is inclined slightly forward; without dropping the chin, look downward. Body inclines slightly forward.

PASSÉ TO FIFTH POSITION SUR LES POINTES—COUNT *eight* (SUSTAINED): Remaining sur la pointe on right leg, raise left foot to retiré in front of right knee and close fifth position front sur les pointes croisé. On the retiré, arms rise upward through second position to third position en haut with the wrists crossed, the left wrist over the right wrist. Then arms move downward in front of the body, with the elbows bending and straightening en bas, the wrists remaining crossed. Head turns left; look downward. Body faces corner 2.

TWO

This combination moves from side to side and then toward corner 4.

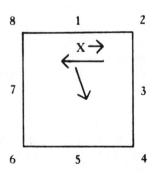

GLISSADE DERRIÈRE TO RIGHT SIDE—COUNT *and:* Demi-plié on the left foot, bringing right foot sur le cou-de-pied back, and glissade to the right side, finishing with right foot back in fifth position demi-plié (no change). Arms are in preparatory position. Body faces front; look toward corner 2.

PIQUÉ ATTITUDE CROISÉE DERRIÈRE—COUNT *one:* Dégagé with the right leg to the side and piqué slightly in front of the body onto the right pointe, at the same time raising the left leg croisé back in attitude position. Body turns slightly to the left on the piqué to face corner 8. Arms pass through first position front as left arm moves upward to third position en haut and right arm opens to second position. Body faces corner 8. Look toward corner 2.

BALANCE WITH PORT-DE-BRAS—COUNT *two* (SUSTAINED): Balancing sur la pointe in attitude croisée derrière, move the right arm inward to first position en avant. Head and body remain the same.

GLISSADE DERRIÈRE TO LEFT SIDE; PIQUÉ ATTITUDE CROISÉE DERRIÈRE—COUNT *and, three:* Tombé to the side on the left leg in demi-plié, bringing the right foot front demi-plié and raising the left foot sur le cou-de-pied back. Repeat count *and, one* to the opposite side.

BALANCE WITH PORT-DE-BRAS—COUNT *four* (SUSTAINED): Same as count *two,* but done to the opposite side.

PAS DE BOURRÉE COURU EN CINQUIÈME EN ARRIÈRE—COUNT *and five, six, and seven:* Remaining sur la pointe on the left leg, close right leg fifth position back sur les pointes and execute ten tiny steps moving to side 5 straight backward while facing the audience. Back leg leads by relaxing and straightening the knee while stepping out to the back. The right arm moves forward and downward to meet the left arm in first position en avant. The left arm moves forward and the right arm moves backward, while relaxing and straightening the elbows, into second position épaulé, left shoulder forward. Body inclines slightly forward; look over left shoulder.

FOURTH POSITION—COUNT *and, eight:* From fifth position sur les pointes, open left leg forward to fourth position front demi-plié (plié à quart), with right leg back with knee straight and foot flat on the floor. Arms move forward to front of body en bas with the left wrist crossed over the right wrist. Head turns and inclines toward the left shoulder. Body faces corner 2.

THREE

Repeat combination ONE exactly.

FOUR*

This combination moves from side to side, and ends at corner 4.

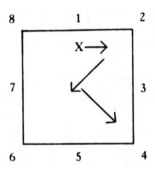

GLISSADE DERRIÈRE TO RIGHT SIDE—COUNT *and:* Demi-plié on left
foot, bringing the right foot sur le cou-de-pied back, and glissade
to the right side, finishing left foot front in fifth position demi-plié
(no change). Arms are in preparatory position. Body faces front.
Look toward corner 2.

PIQUÉ ARABESQUE EFFACÉ—COUNT *one, two* (SUSTAINED): Turn
the body to the right, while bringing the right foot sur le cou-de-
pied back. Step onto the right foot in piqué while raising the
left leg back in arabesque effacée. Right arm moves forward as
in first arabesque position, with the head leaning toward the
right shoulder. Hold balance through count *two.*

* *This combination is similar to combination FOUR of the Sugar Plum Fairy
variation.*

Tombé front changing direction of the body, glissade derrière
to left toward side 7—count *and:* Fall forward onto the
left foot, at the same time changing direction of body to face
corner 6, body is in fourth position demi-plié. Turn body to
right to face corner 8 and, with a slight swivel into fifth position,
bring the right foot front demi-plié. Glissade left, finishing with
right foot front in fifth position demi-plié (no change). Arms are
in preparatory position. Body is facing front; look toward corner 8.

Piqué arabesque effacée—count *three, four* (sustained): Turn
the body to the left, while bringing left foot sur le cou-de-pied
back, and step onto the left pointe in piqué while raising the
right leg back in arabesque effacée. The left arm moves forward
as in first arabesque position with the head leaning toward the
left shoulder. Hold balance through count *four.*

Glissade derrière to right—count *and:* Demi-plié on the left
foot, with right leg dégagé back, and glissade to the right (side
3). Finish with the left foot front in fifth position demi-plié (no
change), turning body to right to face side 3. Arms are in preparatory position. Look toward side 3.

Piqué arabesque with a half-turn en dedans—count
five: Turn the body to the right to face corner 4. With a
demi-plié on the left foot, bring right foot sur le cou-de-pied
back and piqué onto the right pointe toward corner 4, executing
a half-turn to the right so that body finishes facing corner 8.
Arms are in first arabesque position. Look in the direction the
body is going.

Fifth position sur les pointes—count *six:* Remaining sur la
pointe on the right leg, close left foot back to fifth position sur les
pointes. Arms move to second position. Body and head face
corner 8.

Pas de bourrée en tournant sur place—count *and, seven:*
Continue turning to the right in fifth position sur les pointes
two times in place, finishing facing corner 8. Arms move up and
down in second position, relaxing and straightening the elbows.
Head is turned slightly to the right.

Passé to fifth position sur les pointes—count *and,*
eight: Remaining sur la pointe on the right leg, lift left leg to
retiré front of right knee and immediately close to fifth position

front croisé, changing the direction of the body to face corner 2. Arms move upward to third position en haut, with the left wrist crossed over the right wrist, then come down in front of the body, bending the elbows and straightening them en bas, left wrist remaining crossed over the right wrist. The head turns and inclines to the left shoulder; look downward.

FIVE†

This combination moves on a diagonal from corner 4 toward corner 8.

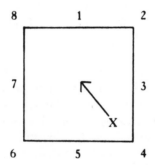

SISSONNE FERMÉE EN AVANT EFFACÉE—COUNT *and, one:* Demi-plié in fifth position and spring forward and upward off both feet, raising the right leg back dégagé (45°). Come down first on the left leg in demi-plié, immediately followed by the right leg back in fifth position demi-plié. Arms extend in front of the body with the left arm higher than the right arm with the palms facing downward; then on the demi-plié in fifth position, the elbows bend and move in toward the body; at the same time the palms of the hands move upward from the wrists. Head and body face corner 8.

SISSONNE FAILLI INTO FOURTH POSITION CROISÉ—COUNT *and, two:* Spring upward and forward off both feet, raising the right leg back dégagé (45°). Come down first on the left leg in demi-plié, immediately followed by the right leg, which passes through first position demi-plié and slides forward into fourth position front croisé in demi-plié. Arms move upward to third position en haut on the sissonne. On the failli, they open outward to

† *For two other versions of this combination, see notes following this variation.*

extend in second position slightly back of the shoulder line, with elbows straight and palms facing downward.

PAS DE BOURRÉE COURU IN FIRST POSITION—COUNT *and:* Step forward onto the left pointe and run forward two quick steps in first position sur les pointes toward corner 8. Arms remain stretched back. Body and head incline forward with the chin raised slightly; look downward toward the floor.

POINTE TENDUE FRONT À TERRE—COUNT *three:* Step forward on the left foot into demi-plié, sliding the right foot through first position demi-plié forward into pointe tendue croisée on the floor, pointing toward corner 8. Arms pass through second position to third position en haut, with hands crossed right over left, and then move downward to extend in front of the body, with the right wrist crossed over the left wrist. Body and head incline forward toward the right leg.

RELEVÉ PASSÉ INTO ARABESQUE EFFACÉE—COUNT *four* (SUSTAINED): Relevé onto the left pointe, at the same time raising the right leg. Bend the right knee so that the foot passes the side of the left knee as it moves back to establish the balance in attitude back effacé (with a passing movement). Continue into arabesque back effacé by straightening the right knee. Arms move upward with hands crossed, right over left, to third position en haut until the attitude position is reached. Then bend the elbows and bringing the hands toward the shoulders push downward and back with the hands (keeping the elbows bent) until the arms extend behind the body in second position. Try to hold the balance in this position, closing the right foot back into fifth position demi-plié at the last moment.

SISSONNE FERMÉE EN AVANT EFFACÉE—COUNT *and, five:* Same as count *and, one.*

SISSONNE FAILLI INTO FOURTH POSITION CROISÉ—COUNT *and, six:* Same as count *and, two.*

PAS DE BOURRÉE COURU IN FIRST POSITION; POINTE TENDUE FRONT À TERRE—COUNT *and, seven:* Same as count *and, three.*

RELEVÉ PASSÉ INTO ARABESQUE EFFACÉE—COUNT *eight* (SUSTAINED): Same as count *four,* but followed by a tombé forward with the right leg passing through first position demi-plié to fourth position front demi-plié. Bring the left foot sur le cou-de-pied back. Arms move to first position en avant. Left arm opens to second position. Head and body incline right.

SIX

This combination moves from side to side, and ends at corner 6.

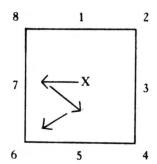

Repeat combination FOUR to the opposite side.

SEVEN

This combination moves on a diagonal from corner 6 toward corner 2.

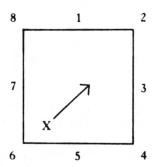

Repeat combination FIVE to the opposite side except that count *eight* ends with a demi-plié on the right leg. The left leg is extended back in arabesque effacée. Arms are extended back, body and head incline back.

EIGHT

This combination moves from side to side, and then to corner 6.

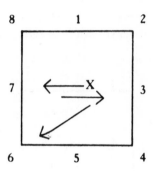

Repeat combination TWO through count *four* to the opposite side. Continue as follows:

TOMBÉ ON LEFT FOOT—COUNT *and:*   Fall to the side onto the left foot facing corner 8 with a demi-plié. Right leg is dégagé back. The left arm moves downward to meet the right arm in first position en avant. Body and head face corner 8.

TEMPS LEVÉ—COUNT *five:*   Jump up off the left foot with right leg dégagé back. Arms open to first arabesque position with left arm front. Body and head are facing corner 8.

TOMBÉ—COUNT *six:*   Fall forward on the right leg, which passes through first position into fourth position croisé front demi-plié, bringing the left foot pointe tendue back and straightening the right knee. Left arm moves over the head with the bent elbow, and the right arm moves front to curve around the front of the waist. Body faces corner 8. Head inclines and turns toward the right shoulder.

WALK GRACEFULLY AND QUICKLY TOWARD CORNER 6—COUNT *and, seven:*   Walk gracefully sur les demi-pointes toward corner 6, step on left foot, right foot, pointing the toes slightly. Arms remain the same as in count *six*. Body and head face in direction of corner 6.

POINTE TENDUE CROISÉE WITH RIGHT FOOT FRONT—COUNT *and, eight:*
Step on the left foot, turning the body to the right to face front as
the right foot moves to pointe tendue front croisé with knees
straight. Arms remain the same as in count *six*. Look right toward corner 2.

NINE‡

This combination moves on the diagonal from corner 6
toward corner 2 to center stage and then back to corner 6.

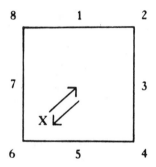

PIQUÉ TOUR EN DEHORS—COUNT *and, one:* Step forward onto the
right foot in demi-plié, at the same time bringing the left foot
dégagé to the side (25°). Step on the left pointe, at the same
time turning to the right and bringing the right foot to retiré in
front of left knee. The right opens to the side. Then both arms
move upward through second position and rise above shoulder
level extended allongé with elbows straight, wrists extended and
palms facing downward. Body faces corner 2; head spots toward
corner 2.

PIQUÉ TOUR EN DEHORS—COUNT *and, two:* Same as count *and, one,*
except that the right arm opens to second position and then both
arms meet in first position en avant.

‡ *Because the recommended recording is too fast, the piqué tours en dehors
in combinations* NINE, TEN, ELEVEN, *and* TWELVE *can be done in half-time.
(One turn is done to every two counts of music.) This shortens the diagonal, an
advantage in a small studio or on a small stage.*

Pas de bourrée couru
en arrière

Piqué tour en dehors—count *and, three:* Same as count *and, one.*

Piqué tour en dehors—count *and, four:* Same as count *and, one,* except that the right arm opens to second position and then both arms meet in first position en avant.

Tombé forward—count *and, five:* Fall forward onto the right foot, bringing the left foot sur le cou-de-pied back. The right arm is in first position en avant; left arm is in second position. Body and head incline to the right, facing corner 2.

Pas de bourrée couru en cinquième en arrière—count *and six, and seven:* Step back onto the left pointe, bringing the right foot front fifth position sur les pointes, and bourrée backward with four tiny steps toward corner 6 while facing front to corner 2. Body faces effacé toward corner 2 with arms in second position, right shoulder forward. The arms move gradually upward, bending and straightening the elbows with a flowing movement of the wrists. Body and head incline toward the right.

POSE IN FIFTH POSITION SUR LES POINTES—COUNT *and, eight:* Remain in fifth position croisé with the right foot front. The left arm moves upward to curve over the head, the right arm curves around in front of body at waist with palm downward. Head inclines to the right; look toward corner 2.

TEN

Repeat combination NINE exactly.

ELEVEN

This combination moves from corner 6 to center stage.

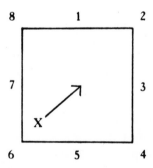

Repeat combination NINE through count *and, four,* except that arms just open to second position and close to first position en avant during the four piqué tours en dehors.

PAS DE BOURRÉE COURU EN CINQUIÈME EN TOURNANT—COUNT *and five, and six, and seven:* Remaining on left pointe, close right foot to fifth position front sur les pointes and bourrée in place, turning to the right with three half-turns. On the first half-turn, the arms move upward in second position; on the second half-turn, the arms move downward in second position; on the third half-turn, the arms move upward again, all with the relaxing and straightening movement of the elbows, as before. (If the stage is large enough, begin the bourrées from a glissade sur les pointes forward toward corner 2.)

POSE IN FIFTH POSITION SUR LES POINTES—COUNT *and, eight:* Same as combination NINE—COUNT *and, eight.*

TWELVE

This combination continues the diagonal from center stage to corner 2. The tempo accelerates.

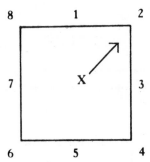

FOUR PIQUÉS TOURS EN DEHORS—COUNT *and one, and two, and three, and four:* Same as combination NINE—count *and, one* through *and, four.*

TWO CHAÎNÉS-DÉBOULÉS TOURS—COUNT *and five, and six:* Demi-plié on left leg and at the same time dégagé right foot front toward corner 2. Step forward onto the right pointe and execute two chaîné-déboulé turns toward corner 2. On first chaîné turn, the right arm opens to second; then both arms come front and remain there for the remainder of the turns. Head spots to corner 2.

STEP ON RIGHT FOOT, STEP ON LEFT FOOT—COUNT *and, seven:* Fall forward onto the right foot into demi-plié, with left foot in low dégagé back effacé, and quickly step forward into demi-plié on the left foot, stepping over in front of the right foot. At the same time bring the right foot sur le cou-de-pied back. Arms are in first position en avant. Body and head face corner 2.

PIQUÉ ARABESQUE—COUNT *and, eight:* Piqué onto the right pointe toward corner 2 and raise the left leg back in arabesque effacée. Arms rise up to second position allongé above shoulder level. Body and head face corner 2.

FOURTH POSITION POINTE TENDUE (FINAL POSE): From arabesque position, left leg passes through first position demi-plié and continues front to fourth position demi-plié. Immediately straighten the left knee and pointe tendue right foot croisé back with knee bent (knees are together). Arms move downward to front of body en bas with left wrist crossed over the right wrist. Body and head incline left. Look toward audience.

Notes

ALTERNATE NO. 1:

FIVE

This combination moves on a diagonal from corner 4 toward corner 8, ending at center stage (for a small stage).

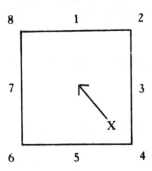

SISSONNE FERMÉE EN AVANT EFFACÉE—COUNT *and, one:* Demi-plié in fifth position and spring upward and forward, raising the right leg back dégagé (45°). Come down first on the left leg in demi-plié, immediately followed by the right leg back in fifth position demi-plié. Arms are in second position with the left shoulder forward. Raise and lower arms by straightening and relaxing elbows, as before. Head and body face corner 8.

SISSONNE FERMÉE EN AVANT EFFACÉE—COUNT *and, two:* Same as count *and, one.*

GLISSADE EN AVANT INTO POINTE TENDUE FRONT À TERRE—COUNT *and, three:* Glissade forward toward corner 8 with the left foot, bringing the right foot through first position demi-plié and sliding it along the floor to pointe tendue front croisé on the floor, remaining in demi-plié on the left foot. Arms rise over the head, with the right wrist crossed over the left wrist, and pass forward and downward to waist level extended in front of the body. Body faces corner 8. Head and body incline forward toward the right leg.

RELEVÉ PASSÉ INTO ARABESQUE EFFACÉE—COUNT *four* (SUSTAINED): Relevé onto the left pointe. At the same time raise the right leg and bend the knee so that the foot passes the side of the left knee as the foot moves back to establish the balance in attitude back effacé, and then continues into arabesque back effacé by straightening the right knee. Arms rise over the head with the wrists still crossed as body straightens in attitude position. For the arabesque, arms come down to the sides, with elbows bent, and continue moving back behind the body as elbows straighten, body and head incline backward. Close right foot back in fifth position at the last moment.

SISSONNE FERMÉE EN AVANT EFFACÉE—COUNT *and, five:* Same as count *and, one.*

SISSONNE FERMÉE EN AVANT EFFACÉE—COUNT *and, six:* Same as count *and, one.*

GLISSADE EN AVANT INTO POINTE TENDUE FRONT À TERRE—COUNT *and, seven:* Same as count *and, three.*

RELEVÉ PASSÉ INTO ARABESQUE EFFACÉE—COUNT *eight*
(SUSTAINED): Same as count *four*. Then tombé forward, with
the right leg passing through first position demi-plié to fourth
position front demi-plié. Bring the left foot sur le cou-de-pied
back, instead of closing right foot back in fifth position demi-plié.
Arms move to front of body wth right wrist crossed over the left
wrist. Body faces corner 8. Head and body incline to the right.

ALTERNATE NO. 2:

This combination was given by Madame Shollar and seems to be a
very early version of the choreography that was later replaced with
combination FIVE as notated above.

PREPARATION

The preceding combination, FOUR, through count *five,* ends at corner
4 in a piqué arabesque with a half-turn en dedans and continues as
follows:

COUNT *six:* Fall back onto the left foot in fourth position demi-plié
with right foot front croisé. Arms pass through preparatory position into first position en avant. Body faces corner 8.

COUNT *and, seven, and, eight:* Then straighten the knees with right
leg pointe tendue front croisé. Left arm rises allongé en haut with
the right arm opening to second position. Body and head incline
to the right.

FIVE

*This combination moves on a diagonal from
corner 4 toward corner 8.*

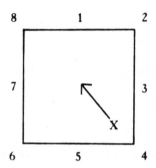

BRISÉ EN AVANT—COUNT *and, one:*   Step forward into demi-plié on
the right foot in fourth position and battement front with the left
foot through first position, at the same time springing up off the
right foot and beating it behind the left foot, which is in the air.
Close right foot front in fifth position demi-plié. The left arm is
in first position en avant with the right arm in second position.
Body faces corner 8 and inclines slightly to the left; look over the
left arm.

RELEVÉ-RETIRÉ—COUNT *and, two:*   Relevé on the left pointe, at the
same time raising the right foot to the front of the left knee in
retiré. The right arm moves to first position en avant as the left
arm moves to second position. Body and head face corner 8.

PIROUETTE EN DEHORS FROM FIFTH POSITION—COUNT *and:*   Relevé
on the left pointe and turn to the right, raising the right foot
front in retiré with a single or double turn. Right arm opens and
then meets the left arm in first position en avant. Body faces
corner 8. Head spots to corner 8.

DÉVELOPPÉ RIGHT LEG À LA QUATRIÈME DEVANT CROISÉ—COUNT
three: Remaining sur la pointe on the left leg, open the right

foot front in the air at least 90° or over. Both arms rise up and extend to the side in second position, higher than shoulder level, with elbows straight in allongé position, palms downward and extended. Body and head face corner 8. Chin is raised slightly.

Tombé forward into fourth position—count *four* (sustained): Fall forward onto the right foot into fourth position demi-plié croisé. Arms move outward and downward with the right arm moving to second position and the left arm continuing through preparatory position to first position en avant. Body and head incline toward left; look over the left arm.

Brisé en avant—count *and, five:* Same as count *and, one.*

Relevé-retiré—count *and, six:* Same as count *and, two.*

Pirouette en dehors from fifth position; développé right leg à la quatrième devant croisé—count *and, seven:* Same as count *and, three.*

Fifth position sur les pointes—count *eight* (sustained): Remaining sur la pointe, close the right foot front fifth position sur les pointes. Arms remain in second position extended, with the left arm slightly higher than shoulder level. Body faces corner 8; look toward audience.

SWAN QUEEN'S
ACT II CODA

From the Ballet

Le Lac des Cygnes

Margot Fonteyn and Rudolf Nureyev
as the Swan Queen Odette and Siegfried in SWAN LAKE.

———————————————————

Natalia Makarova and Ivan Nagy

as the Swan Queen Odette and Prince Siegfried in SWAN LAKE.

SWAN QUEEN'S
ACT II CODA

Prima ballerina coda ending from the Act II Coda of *The Swan Lake* ballet. MUSIC by Peter Ilyich Tchaikovsky. CHOREOGRAPHY by Lev Ivanov. AS TAUGHT by Anatole Vilzak and Barbara Fallis. NOTATED AND ADAPTED by Laurencia Klaja. TEMPO 6/8, allegro vivace.

Recommended Recordings

1. *Swan Lake Ballet Suite*. New York Philharmonic, conducted by Leonard Bernstein. Columbia Records/CBS, Columbia Masterworks, STEREO M-30056. Side 1, Act II. Last selection, marked "Coda." Begin dancing on the third set of eight counts.

2. *Tchaikovsky. The Swan Lake Ballet* (Excerpts) *Three Great Tchaikovsky Ballets*. The Philadelphia Orchestra, conducted by Eugene Ormandy. Columbia Records, Columbia Masterworks, STEREO D3S-706. Side II. Second selection, Coda. Follows "Danses des Petits Cygnes" (Pas de Quatre).

Piano Music

Le Lac des Cygnes (*The Swan Lake*), by Peter Ilyich Tchaikovsky. Opus 20. Grand Ballet in Four Acts. Act II, No. 17, Coda, page 84.

Begin dancing on the third set of eight counts. (The music changes for the entrechat-quatre–relevé passé combination.) Published by The Tschaikovsky Foundation, 1950.

Comments

Classical pas de deux usually contain a short coda or finale at a fast tempo that shows off the technique of the dancer. The following Coda from Act II of *The Swan Lake* ballet is one of these. (A more difficult coda is the Black Swan Pas de Deux of Act III in the same ballet that includes the famous thirty-two fouettés.)

It is worthwhile to become proficient in this sort of tour de force, which, besides being very exciting to the audience, is an obvious test of the dancer's skill and, if done well, should also bring down the house with applause.

INTRODUCTION

The sixteen bar melody, repeated twice, brings in the corps de ballet and soloists, and finally as a grand climax, the Swan Queen enters, on the third repeat, at upper stage left (corner 6). The ballerina quickly assumes the first pose.

PREPARATORY POSE WITH RIGHT FOOT FRONT CROISÉ POINTE TENDUE. The right arm is in first position en avant with the left arm in second position. Look toward downstage right corner 2.

ONE

This combination moves diagonally from corner 6 toward corner 2.

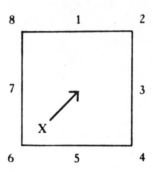

P<small>IQUÉ INTO GRAND FOUETTÉ EN TOURNANT</small>—<small>COUNT</small> *and, one:* With
a demi-plié on the left leg, piqué forward onto the right pointe
toward corner 2. The left leg passes through first position forward to fourth position front at 45°. While remaining on the
right pointe, turn the body to the right so that the left leg rises to
second position (90°). At the same time turn in the hip joint
into fourth arabesque position croisé, facing diagonally back
toward corner 6. The arms pass through preparatory position to
first position en avant before opening strongly to fourth arabesque
position, with the right arm extended front. (Body finishes in
arabesque with left leg back and head facing corner 6.)

G<small>LISSADE PRESSÉE</small>—<small>COUNT</small> *and, two:* From arabesque position,
body continues turning to the right as the left leg closes back in
fifth position demi-plié facing front. Glissade to the side toward
corner 2 without changing the feet. (This may be done without
lowering the right heel to the floor, keeping the right pointe extended on the floor during the glissade.)

P<small>IQUÉ INTO GRAND FOUETTÉ EN TOURNANT</small>—<small>COUNT</small> *and, three:*
Same as count *and, one.*

G<small>LISSADE PRESSÉE</small>—<small>COUNT</small> *and, four:* Same as count *and, two.*

*Piqué into grand fouetté
en tournant*

PIQUÉ INTO GRAND FOUETTÉ EN TOURNANT—COUNT *and, five:* Same as count *and, one.*

GLISSADE PRESSÉE—COUNT *and, six:* Same as count *and, two.*

PIQUÉ INTO GRAND FOUETTÉ EN TOURNANT—COUNT *and, seven:* Same as count *and, one.*

GLISSADE PRESSÉE—COUNT *and, eight:* Same as count *and, two.*

TWO

*This combination continues the diagonal toward corner 2
and ends with a run around to the left to center stage.*

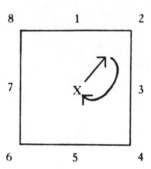

PIQUÉ INTO GRAND FOUETTÉ EN TOURNANT—COUNT *and, one:* Same
as combination ONE—count *and, one.*

GLISSADE PRESSÉE—COUNT *and, four:* Same as combination ONE—
count *and, two.*

PIQUÉ INTO GRAND FOUETTÉ EN TOURNANT—COUNT *and, three:* Same
as combination ONE—count *and, one.*

GLISSADE PRESSÉE—COUNT *and, four:* Same as combination ONE—
count *and, two.*

PIQUÉ INTO GRAND FOUETTÉ EN TOURNANT—COUNT *and, five:* Same
as combination *one*—count *and, one.* Hold arabesque position on
count *five.*

TOMBÉ INTO TEMPS LEVÉ—COUNT *and, six:* Fall forward onto the
left foot into fourth position front effacé demi-plié, with right leg
dégagé back (45°) facing side 7. Jump up into the air off the
left foot with right leg dégagé back. Arms move to first arabesque
position with left arm front. Body and head face side 7.

RUN SUR LES DEMI-POINTES—COUNT *and, seven:* Step forward onto
the right foot and run to stage center front in double time—right

foot, left foot, right foot, left foot—changing the direction of the
body to face front. Arms are in demi-seconde position slightly
back of the body.

Assemblé to fifth position en face—count *and, eight:* With
the left foot forward in demi-plié, brush the right foot front
(25°), jumping up on the left foot, and close in fifth position
demi-plié with the right foot front, facing the audience. (This
assemblé gives speed and force to the next combination, which
follows without a pause.) Arms close to preparatory position.
Body and head face front, en face.

THREE

*This combination moves straight back at center
stage facing front. The tempo is very fast.*

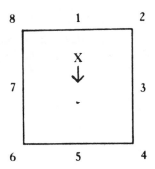

Entrechat-quatre—count *one:* With a small jump upward off
both feet, quickly interchange the legs in the air, beating the
calves together, and come down, without changing feet, into fifth
position demi-plié with the right foot front. (Accent is down.)
Arms are in low second position at the sides. Body and head
remain facing audience.

Relevé passé back—count *two:* Spring onto the left pointe and
quickly raise the right foot to a low retiré between the knee and
ankle. Come down in fifth position demi-plié with the right foot
back. (Accent is down.) Both arms rise and lower at the sides
with elbows relaxed. The wrists are up and the palms down
when arms move upward, and the wrists are down and the

palms up when arms move downward, like the movement of a bird's wings. Body faces front to audience as before. Look toward corner 2.

ENTRECHAT-QUATRE—COUNT *three:*   Same as count *one,* but done to the opposite side.

RELEVÉ PASSÉ BACK—COUNT *four:*   Same as count *two,* but done to the opposite side.

RELEVÉ PASSÉ BACK—COUNT *five:*   Same as count *two,* except that the arms will continue to move upward. Head and body face the audience.

RELEVÉ PASSÉ BACK—COUNT *six:*   Same as count *two,* but done to the opposite side. Arms should have reached third position en haut with wrists crossed over the head.

RELEVÉ PASSÉ BACK—COUNT *seven:*   Same as count *two,* except that arms begin to move downward in front of the body with the wrists crossed.

RELEVÉ PASSÉ BACK—COUNT *eight:*   Same as count *two,* but done to the opposite side. Arms have reached the front of waist with the wrists crossed.

FOUR

This combination continues moving back at center stage.

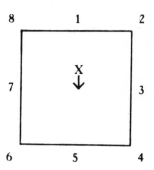

Repeat combination THREE exactly.

FIVE

This combination continues moving back at stage center.

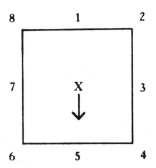

ENTRECHAT-QUATRE—COUNT *one:* Same as combination THREE— count *one.*

RELEVÉ PASSÉ BACK—COUNT *two:* Same as combination THREE— count *two.*

ENTRECHAT-QUATRE—COUNT *three:* Same as combination THREE— count *one,* but done to the opposite side.

RELEVÉ PASSÉ BACK—COUNT *four:* Same as combination THREE— count *two,* but done to the opposite side.

SOUS-SUS SUR LES POINTES IN FIFTH POSITION—COUNT *five:* Relevé on both pointes in fifth position in place with the right foot front croisé. The right arm curves across the front of body at waist; the left arm is raised above the head with the elbow bent so that it curves gracefully around the head without actually touching it. The épaulement of the body is croisé. Look toward corner 2.

HOLD POSE FIFTH POSITION SUR LES POINTES—COUNT *six* (SUS-TAINED): Remain in fifth position sur les pointes with arms and body the same as for count *five.*

SIX

This combination moves on a diagonal from back of center stage toward corner 2 in a series of fast turns.

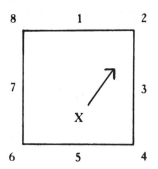

PIQUÉ TOUR EN DEHORS—COUNT *one:* Step forward into demi-plié on the right leg toward corner 2 and, with a dégagé to the side (25°) with the left leg, step onto the left pointe, turning to the right and bringing the right foot retiré front. The right arm swings outward toward second position followed by a swing inward with the left arm, which then meets the right arm in first position en avant. Head spots to corner 2.

PIQUÉ TOUR EN DEHORS—COUNT *two:* Same as count *one.*

PIQUÉ TOUR EN DEHORS—COUNT *three:* Same as count *one.*

PIQUÉ TOUR EN DEHORS—COUNT *four:* Same as count *one.*

THREE CHAÎNÉS-DÉBOULÉS TOURS—COUNT *five, six, seven:* Demi-plié on the left leg and dégagé right foot front, immediately stepping forward onto the right pointe and executing three quick chaîné-déboulé turns to the right sur les pointes in first position. Finish the last turn facing corner 2 with a demi-plié on the left foot, right foot dégagé front. The right arm swings outward on first chaîné turn with the left arm closing to meet it in first position en avant, where they remain for the remaining turns. Head spots to corner 2.

Pointe tendue

POINTE TENDUE (FINAL POSE)—COUNT *eight:* Step forward onto the right foot flat and pointe tendue the left foot back on the floor in a position that is in between fourth position effacé and second position. Both arms open outward to second position. The right arm continues upward to curve over the head as the left arm moves inward to curve around the waist. The left shoulder is forward. Look to the left over the left shoulder with the eyes cast downward.

SYLVIA'S
WALTZ VARIATION

From the Ballet

Sylvia

ou La Nymphe de Diane
[or The Nymph of Diana]

Maria Tallchief

in George Balanchine's SYLVIA PAS DE DEUX.

———————————————

SYLVIA'S WALTZ VARIATION

Prima ballerina variation from Act III of the ballet *Sylvia*. MUSIC by Léo Delibes. CHOREOGRAPHY possibly by Lev Ivanov after Louis Mérante. AS TAUGHT by Ludmilla Shollar and Anatole Vilzak. NO-TATED by Laurencia Klaja. TEMPO 3/4, waltz.

Recommended Recording

Sylvia. Complete ballet by Léo Delibes. Conducted by Jean-Baptiste Mari, with the Paris Opera Orchestra. Angel Records, NUMBER SB-3860. Side 4: Sixth selection, Waltz.

Piano Music

Act III. Waltz Variation (*Sylvia*). Follows "Pas des Esclaves" (Dance of the Slaves) in the complete score. The music for this variation was interpolated into Act III of Delibes's *Coppélia* for Franz's variation as done by the New York City Ballet, because no variation had been written into it for the male dancer since at that period of time he was at his nadir. The role of Franz was originally danced by a woman impersonating a man (en travesti) and this practice continued in the Paris Opera Ballet as late as the 1950s. Since the score for the ballet *Sylvia* is not readily available, the piano music from the first edition is being included in this book.

Comments

A Milanese ballerina, Rita Sangalli, was the first Sylvia, on June 14, 1876, when the ballet was premiered at the Paris Opera House. The choreographer, Louis Mérante, danced the role of Aminta, the shepherd in love with the nymph, Sylvia, a follower of the chaste goddess Diana, the huntress. *Sylvia, ou, La Nymphe de Diane* used a libretto taken from a mythological story about gods and goddesses, a favorite theme for early ballets. The first Russian production was given in St. Petersburg in 1901 with choreography by Lev Ivanov (who died before the ballet was completed) and Pavel Gerdt, premier danseur of the Maryinsky Theatre. Frederick Ashton choreographed a version for Margot Fonteyn in 1952. George Balanchine choreographed a *Sylvia Pas de Deux*.

This variation takes place in Act III. It celebrates the reunion of the shepherd Aminta with Sylvia after her abduction by the evil hunter, Orion, and the intervention of the god of love, Eros, to bring them together again.

VARIATION-VALSE.

(SYLVIA)

INTRODUCTION

*From downstage right corner 2, run to upstage
left corner 6, or stand in place.*

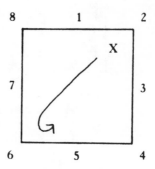

COUNT *one* **THROUGH** *seven:*   When corner 6 is reached, step around
to the left and end facing front to corner 2. Or, just stand in
place at corner 6 for the first seven counts. Arms are in demi-
seconde position.

POINTE TENDUE WITH PORT-DE-BRAS—COUNT *and, eight:*   With a low
bending forward of the body, demi-plié in fourth position à
terre croisé, with the left foot front facing corner 2, straighten
both knees simultaneously and pointe tendue front croisé with
the left foot. At the same time with a very quick movement, both
arms move to third position en haut rounded, passing through
second position, then pass downward to first position front en
avant and, with a strong movement, extend allongé to a high second position above shoulder level with palms extended and
facing upward. (Port-de-bras should be done in a manner that
conveys a feeling of joy.) Look toward arms while they are
moving. On the final pose look toward the audience.

ONE

This combination moves diagonally downstage from corner 6 toward corner 2. This combination should fly!

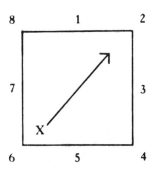

CABRIOLE DEVANT EFFACÉE—COUNT *and:*   Step forward into a strong demi-plié on the left foot, which is front, toward corner 2. Brush the right foot through first position to fourth position effacé front en l'air, executing a cabriole front effacé by beating the left calf under the right calf. The left foot returns to floor in demi-plié while the right leg remains en l'air effacé front. Both arms pass through preparatory position to first position en avant; then the right arm rises to third position en haut rounded as the left arm opens to second position. Look to corner 8.

SMALL JETÉ FORWARD ONTO THE RIGHT FOOT—COUNT *one:*   Pushing off the left foot from demi-plié, jump forward onto the right foot into demi-plié toward corner 2. The left foot is extended back dégagé fourth position effacé (25°). The right arm opens to second position with palm facing upward. Body inclines slightly to the right. Head inclines right; look front toward the audience.

PAS DE BOURRÉE CHANGÉE—COUNT *and, two:*   With a quick movement, left foot draws behind the right foot sur les demi-pointes in fifth position. Remaining sur les demi-pointes, right foot opens to second position à terre. Arms begin to move downward to preparatory position. Body straightens. Look toward corner 2.

Cabriole devant effacée

—Close the left foot front in fourth position croisé with a strong demi-plié on both feet. Arms are in preparatory position; look toward corner 2.

CABRIOLE DEVANT EFFACÉE; SMALL JETÉ FORWARD ONTO THE RIGHT FOOT—COUNT *and, three:* Same as count *and, one,* with right foot brushing through first position immediately with a strong demi-plié on the left foot.

PAS DE BOURRÉE CHANGÉE—COUNT *and, four:* Same as count *and, two.*

CABRIOLE DEVANT EFFACÉE; SMALL JETÉ FORWARD ONTO THE RIGHT FOOT—COUNT *and, five:* Same as count *and, one,* with right foot brushing through first position immediately with a strong demi-plié on the left foot.

PAS DE BOURRÉE CHANGÉE—COUNT *and, six:* Same as count *and, two.*

GLISSADE (NO CHANGE)—COUNT *and, seven:* Glissade to the right side with a dégagé of the right foot to second position à terre, closing the left foot front in fifth position demi-plié en face. Arms open and close slightly to the side. Body and head face front.

DÉGAGÉ FRONT WITH RIGHT FOOT—COUNT *and:* Turning body slightly to the right to face side 3, dégagé the right foot front with demi-plié on the left foot. Arms move up to first position en avant. Body and head face side 3.

PIQUÉ ARABESQUE—COUNT *eight:* Piqué on the right pointe to side 3 and raise the left foot back into first arabesque position. Arms are in first arabesque position with the right arm front. Look toward right wrist.

TWO

This combination moves from side to side and then returns to upstage left corner 6.

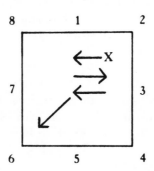

CHASSÉ TO LEFT—COUNT *and, one:* After piqué arabesque, close left leg to fourth position back effacé demi-plié. With a small spring into the air off both feet, change direction of body to face side 7. Come down in fourth position effacé demi-plié with left foot in front. Arms move downward to the sides in low second position. Body and head face side 7.

—Spring off both feet, drawing them together in the air with the left foot in front, and chassé forward to side 7 into fourth position effacé demi-plié with left foot remaining in front. (Be sure the weight of the body is forward.) Arms remain at the sides. Head and body face side 7.

Relevé arabesque—count *and, two:* Making sure that your weight is over the left foot in demi-plié, relevé on the left foot and raise the right leg back in arabesque effacée. Arms rise at the sides upward and then gracefully downward with elbows relaxed. Body and head face side 7.

Chassé to right—count *and, three:* After relevé arabesque, close the right leg to fourth position back effacé demi-plié and, with a small spring into the air off both feet, change direction of body to face side 3. Come down in fourth position effacé demi-plié with the right foot in front. Arms move downward to the sides. Body and head face side 3.

—Spring off both feet, drawing them together in the air with the right foot in front, and chassé forward to side 3 into fourth position effacé demi-plié with the right foot remaining in front. (Be sure the weight of the body is forward.) Arms remain at the sides. Head and body face side 3.

Relevé arabesque—count *and, four:* Making sure that your weight is over the right foot in demi-plié, relevé on the right foot and raise the left leg back in arabesque effacée. Arms rise at the sides upward and then downward gracefully with elbows relaxed. Body and head face side 3.

Chassé to left—count *and:* After relevé arabesque on count *four,* close the left leg to fourth position back effacé demi-plié. With a small spring into the air off both feet, change direction of body to face side 7, coming down in fourth position effacé demi-plié with left foot in front. Arms move downward to preparatory position. Body and head face side 7.

Cabriole derrière—count *five:* Springing up off the left foot in place, raise the right leg back dégagé and beat the left calf under the right calf. Arms move to first arabesque position allongé with the left arm extended front, with elbow straight and palm stretched out and facing downward. The left arm is higher than shoulder level, while the right arm is back lower than shoulder level. Body and head face side 7; look toward left wrist.

TOMBÉ FRONT ON RIGHT FOOT—COUNT *six:* Come down in demi-plié on right foot front, bringing the left foot sur le cou-de-pied back, with a slight pause. The left arm moves downward to second as the right arm moves front en avant. Body inclines slightly to right; look toward audience.

RUN TO UPSTAGE CORNER 6—COUNT *seven:* Run gracefully and quickly sur les demi-pointes toward upstage corner 6. After reaching corner 6, step to the left so as to face front to corner 2. Arms are held gracefully, slightly away from the sides. Look in the direction that one is going.

PORT-DE-BRAS WITH POINTE TENDUE FRONT—COUNT *and, eight:* Step back onto the right foot in demi-plié and pointe tendue left foot croisé front as the right knee straightens in preparatory pose as at the beginning of the variation. Arms rise to first position en avant; first the right arm opens forward toward the right with palm turning upward, and then the left arm opens forward toward the left with the palm opening upward. Look toward right arm first, then look toward left arm and audience.

THREE

Repeat combination ONE exactly.

FOUR

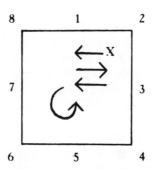

Repeat combination TWO, but on count *seven,* run left and then around to the right side and finish at center stage instead of at corner 6 for count *and, eight.*

FIVE

This combination moves back and then diagonally forward to the right toward corner 2.

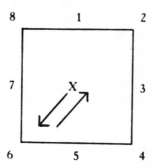

TOMBÉ FORWARD—COUNT *and:* Fall forward onto the left foot, transferring the weight forward, and bring the right foot sur le cou-de-pied back. Arms move to preparatory position. Body and head incline slightly forward.

CHASSÉ BACK—COUNT *one:* With a small spring on the left foot, slide the right foot diagonally backward into demi-plié on the right foot, bringing the left foot sur le cou-de-pied front. Arms move to first position en avant. Body straightens and then inclines to the right. Head turns and inclines to the right.

RELEVÉ-DÉVELOPPÉ FRONT CROISÉ—COUNT *two:* Relevé on the right pointe, at the same time opening the left leg croisé front en l'air (90°) with a développé in the direction of corner 2. The left foot closes front fifth position croisé demi-plié. Arms pass through first position en avant as the right arm rises to third position rounded en haut and the left arm opens to second position. Body and head incline to the left. Head looks toward audience.

GLISSADE (NO CHANGE)—COUNT *and:* The right foot opens to the side with glissade to the right to corner 2, closing the left foot front fifth position demi-plié. Arms move outward and downward to preparatory position. Body straightens; looks toward corner 2.

ASSEMBLÉ BATTU OR ENTRECHAT-SIX DE VOLÉ—COUNT *three:*   With the momentum gained from the preceding glissade, spring off the left foot and thrust the right leg à la seconde en l'air, écarté to corner 2. For the assemblé battu, beat the left leg over the right leg and at the moment of alighting, change feet so that the right foot is fifth position front croisé in demi-plié. For entrechat-six de volé, spring off the left foot, thrust the right leg à la seconde en l'air, and immediately beat the left leg first under the right leg. Then, remaining en l'air, quickly open the legs slightly, pass left leg front, and beat calves again before alighting with the right foot front fifth position croisé demi-plié. Arms pass through first position en avant and open. The right arm is extended allongé second position, slightly higher than shoulder level, palm facing downward. The left arm opens to second position, lower than shoulder level, palm facing downward. Look toward corner 2.

FIFTH POSITION DEMI-PLIÉ—COUNT *four:*   Alight with the right foot front fifth position croisé demi-plié. Arms remain in second position allongé. Remain looking toward corner 2.

RELEVÉ-RETIRÉ FRONT—COUNT *and, five:*   With relevé, rise on the left pointe bringing the right foot front of left knee. The left arm remains in second position while the right arm moves downward to preparatory position and rises upward to first position. Body inclines slightly to the right; look over right arm.

—Close right foot front in fifth position croisé demi-plié. Arms, body, and head remain the same.

RELEVÉ PASSÉ BACK—COUNT *six:*   With relevé, rise on the left pointe, bringing the right foot retiré front of the left knee, and immediately close fifth position back demi-plié. This relevé is done twice as fast as the relevé-retiré front of count *and, five.* The left arm remains in second position and the right arm remains in first position en avant. Body remains slightly inclined to the right; look over the right arm.

RELEVÉ PASSÉ FRONT—COUNT *and:*   With relevé, rise on the left pointe, bringing the right foot retiré to front of the left knee. Immediately close fifth position front croisé demi-plié in preparation for the following pirouette from fifth position. Arms remain the same with the left arm in second and the right arm in first position. Body straightens; look toward corner 8.

Pɪʀᴏᴜᴇᴛᴛᴇ ᴇɴ ᴅᴇʜᴏʀs ꜰʀᴏᴍ ꜰɪꜰᴛʜ ᴘᴏsɪᴛɪᴏɴ—ᴄᴏᴜɴᴛ *seven:* With relevé, rise on the left pointe and execute a double (or single) pirouette to the right from fifth position, taking force for the pirouette from the left shoulder. With right arm in first position and left arm in second position, close left arm to first position so that both arms are in first position en avant during the turn. Body is straight; head spots to corner 8.

Fɪꜰᴛʜ ᴘᴏsɪᴛɪᴏɴ ʀɪɢʜᴛ ꜰᴏᴏᴛ ꜰʀᴏɴᴛ—ᴄᴏᴜɴᴛ *eight:* Finish the pirouette, bringing the right foot fifth position front croisé in demi-plié. Arms are in first position en avant. Body is straight.

SIX

This combination moves back and then diagonally forward toward corner 8.

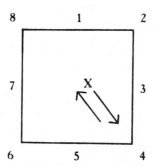

Sɪssᴏɴɴᴇ sɪᴍᴘʟᴇ—ᴄᴏᴜɴᴛ *and:* From fifth position, jump off the right foot in place, raising the left foot sur le cou-de-pied back, coming down on the right foot in demi-plié with the left foot still sur le cou-de-pied back. Arms are in first position front en avant. Body and head incline slightly forward.

Cʜᴀssé ʙᴀᴄᴋ—ᴄᴏᴜɴᴛ *one:* Same as combination ꜰɪᴠᴇ—count *one,* but done to the opposite side.

Relevé-développé front croisé

RELEVÉ-DÉVELOPPÉ FRONT CROISÉ—COUNT *two:* Same as combination—tion FIVE—count *two,* but done to the opposite side.

GLISSADE (NO CHANGE); ASSEMBLÉ BATTU OR ENTRECHAT-SIX DE VOLÉ—COUNT *and, three:* Same as combination FIVE—count *and, three,* but done to the opposite side.

FIFTH POSITION DEMI-PLIÉ—COUNT *four:* Same as combination FIVE —count *four,* but done to the opposite side.

RELEVÉ PASSÉ BACK—COUNT *and:* (The left foot is fifth position front demi-plié.) With a relevé, rise on the right pointe, bring the left foot retiré front of the right knee. Immediately close the left foot fifth position back demi-plié, changing épaulement so that the right foot is croisé front. The right arm remains in second position as the left arm moves downward to preparatory position and rises upward to first position en avant. Body inclines slightly to the left; look over the left arm.

RELEVÉ PASSÉ FRONT—COUNT *five:* With a relevé, rise on the right pointe, bring the left foot retiré front of the right knee. Immediately close the left foot fifth position croisé front demi-plié in preparation for the following pirouette. The left arm remains in first position en avant, with the right arm in second position. Body straightens; look to corner 2.

PIROUETTE EN DEHORS FROM FIFTH POSITION—COUNT *six:* Same as combination FIVE—count *seven,* but done to the left side. The pirouette finishes left foot back fifth position croisé demi-plié.

SEVEN

*This combination moves diagonally back to corner 4,
and is a continuation of combination* SIX.

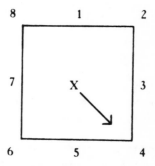

SOUS-SUS SUR LES POINTES SUR PLACE—COUNT *and:* Remaining in place, relevé into fifth position croisé sur les pointes with right foot front. Arms pass through first position en avant to third position en haut rounded. Body faces corner 8 with the left shoulder slightly forward and body inclined slightly to the right. Look toward the audience.

PAS DE BOURRÉE COURU BACKWARD DIAGONALLY TO CORNER 4—COUNT *seven* (DRAWN OUT FOR THREE BEATS): Remaining sur les pointes in fifth position croisé, bourrée backward with the left foot leading the movement by opening back with a tiny step and drawing the right foot toward it for each of the six bourrées in double time. (Two bourrées for each beat.) Arms remain third position en haut rounded en couronne. Body faces corner 8 with shoulders also facing corner 8. Look toward corner 8.

Attitude front croisé

ATTITUDE FRONT CROISÉ—COUNT *eight* (SUSTAINED): (Corner 4 should have been reached.) Remaining sur la pointe on the left leg, raise the right leg to attitude front croisé and hold balance in this position. The right arm opens outward to second position, while the left arm remains in third position en haut rounded. Body inclines slightly to the right with the left shoulder slightly forward. Look right toward the audience.

EIGHT

This combination moves diagonally forward to corner 8.

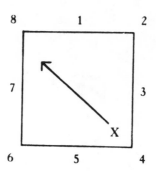

PETIT JETÉ (BATTU) WITH CHANGE OF DIRECTION—COUNT
and: Fall forward toward corner 8 onto the right foot in
demi-plié and bring the left foot back sur le cou-de-pied. Execute a small jeté to the side with the left foot brushing to the left
side in low second position en l'air toward corner 8. Change the
direction of the body to face corner 2. Come down on the left
foot with right foot sur le cou-de-pied back. May also be done
with a battu of the right foot over the left leg while en l'air,
coming down with the right foot sur le cou-de-pied back as
above. Both arms open to second position. Head spots over the
left shoulder toward corner 8.

RELEVÉ-RETIRÉ EN TOURNANT EN DEHORS—COUNT *one:* Spring up
onto the left pointe, at the same time turning to the right to again
face corner 8, bringing the right foot from sur le cou-de-pied
back to retiré front. (The right foot must *not* open front while
the left foot remains on the pointe after the turn, although it has
a tendency to do so.) Both arms close to first position en avant
to give impetus to the turn. As the body turns to the right, head
quickly changes from looking over the left shoulder to looking
over the right shoulder and then front toward corner 8.

PETIT JETÉ (BATTU) WITH CHANGE OF DIRECTION; RELEVÉ-RETIRÉ
EN TOURNANT EN DEHORS—COUNT *and, two:* Same as count
and, one.

PETIT JETÉ (BATTU) WITH CHANGE OF DIRECTION; RELEVÉ-RETIRÉ
EN TOURNANT EN DEHORS—COUNT *and, three:* Same as count
and, one.

PETIT JETÉ (BATTU) WITH CHANGE OF DIRECTION; RELEVÉ-RETIRÉ
EN TOURNANT EN DEHORS—COUNT *and, four:* Same as count
and, one.

PETIT JETÉ (BATTU) WITH CHANGE OF DIRECTION; RELEVÉ-RETIRÉ
EN TOURNANT EN DEHORS—COUNT *and, five:* Same as count
and, one.

PETIT JETÉ (BATTU) WITH CHANGE OF DIRECTION; RELEVÉ-RETIRÉ EN
TOURNANT EN DEHORS—COUNT *and, six:* Same as count *and,
one.*

PETIT ASSEMBLÉ INTO FIFTH POSITION—COUNT *and, seven:* After the
last relevé-retiré, demi-plié on the left foot with the right foot sur
le cou-de-pied front and execute a small assemblé: jump up on
the left foot in place with the right foot sur le cou-de-pied front
and close into fifth position demi-plié with the right foot front
croisé. Arms move downward to preparatory position en bas.
Body faces corner 8.

SOUS-SUS SUR LES POINTES—COUNT *and, eight* (SUSTAINED):
Spring up into a relevé sur les pointes in fifth position in place
with the right foot front croisé and hold pose. Arms pass through
first position en avant to third position rounded en haut. Body
inclines slightly to the right; look front toward audience.

NINE

*This combination moves straight across from left to right
(from side 7 to side 3).*

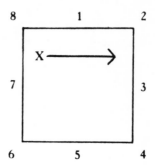

GLISSADE (NO CHANGE)—COUNT *and:* Demi-plié in fifth position, as arms open outward through second position and down to pre-paratory position, and execute a glissade to the right (side 3) with the right foot closing fifth position front demi-plié (without changing feet). Arms are in preparatory position. Head looks to-ward side 3.

SAUT DE BASQUE—COUNT *one, two:* Step forward on the right foot in demi-plié to side 3. Spring off the right foot, thrust the left foot to second position en l'air, changing the direction of the body to face the back. Turning to the right en l'air, come down on the left foot demi-plié with the right foot front sur le cou-de-pied. Arms open to second position on jump and close to first po-sition en avant on demi-plié. Head spots to side 3 on the turn in the air and to front on demi-plié.

SAUT DE BASQUE—COUNT *three, four:* Same as count *one, two.*

GLISSADE (NO CHANGE)—COUNT *and:* (The right foot is sur le cou-de-pied front.) Glissade to the right (side 3) with the right foot closing fifth position front demi-plié (without changing feet).

PIQUÉ TOUR EN DEDANS—COUNT *five:* Dégagé right foot front with demi-plié on the left leg to side 3 and step forward onto the right pointe, bringing the left foot retiré back, and execute a turn to the right. The right arm opens forward and then moves inward to meet the left arm in first position en avant during the turn. Head spots to side 3.

PIQUÉ TOUR EN DEDANS—COUNT *six:* Same as count *five.*

DOUBLE PIQUÉ TOUR EN DEDANS—COUNT *seven:* Same as count *five,* except that instead of a single piqué tour, a double piqué tour is executed.

FIFTH POSITION DEMI-PLIÉ CROISÉ—COUNT *and:* Close the left foot in fifth position front croisé demi-plié. Arms are in first position en avant; look front to audience.

SOUS-SUS SUR LES POINTES—COUNT *eight:* Spring up in place into a relevé sur les pointes in fifth position with the left foot front croisé and hold final pose. Arms pass through first position en avant to third position rounded en haut in final pose. Body inclines slightly to the left with left shoulder slightly forward. Look toward the audience.

Biographies

LUDMILLA SHOLLAR (or Schollar) was born in 1888 in St. Petersburg, Russia, and, in 1906 graduated from the Imperial Ballet School, where she was a pupil of Michel Fokine and Enrico Cecchetti. She was Vaslav Nijinsky's first partner at their graduation performance. Between 1910 and 1914 she divided her time between the Maryinsky Theatre in St. Petersburg and touring with Diaghilev's Ballets Russes. She created roles in the ballets *Carnaval, Scheherazade,* and *Petrouchka,* choreographed by Michel Fokine, and the role of one of the two girls in *Jeux,* choreographed by Vaslav Nijinsky. During World War I while serving as a Red Cross nurse in the Russian army, she was wounded on the front lines and was later decorated with the Medal of St. George for bravery. After the war ended she resumed her dancing career at the Maryinsky Theatre and returned to the Diaghilev company in 1921. She danced the White Cat on opening night of *The Sleeping Beauty* Ballet in London and later danced Princess Florine in the Bluebird Pas de Deux of the same ballet. From 1921 until 1935 she and her husband, Anatole Vilzak, appeared with the Ida Rubinstein Company in Paris, the Karsavina-Vilzak Company in London, and Bronislava Nijinska's company in Paris. In 1935 she retired from dancing and began to teach ballet in New York City. She taught there for twenty-eight years—from 1940 to 1946 at the Vilzak-Schollar School of Ballet and later at the Ballet Theatre School (now the American Ballet Theatre School). She and her husband taught at the Washington School of Ballet in Washington, D.C., from 1963 to 1965, when they moved to San Francisco, where she taught at the San Francisco Ballet School until 1977. She died at the age of ninety in 1978. She was particularly noted for her teaching of classical ballet variations.

Ludmilla Shollar

during a season of the Diaghilev Ballets Russes in Paris

Anatole Vilzak

partners Olga Spessivtzeva in SWAN LAKE

ANATOLE VILZAK was born in St. Petersburg in 1898 and graduated in 1915 from the Imperial Ballet School, where he was a pupil of Michel Fokine. He became premier danseur of the Maryinsky Theatre three years after joining the company, dancing in all the classical ballets of the repertoire. He was the partner of such leading ballerinas as Mathilde Kchessinska, Tamara Karsavina, and Olga Spessivtzeva. He joined Diaghilev's Ballets Russes as premier danseur in 1921. He and his wife, Ludmilla Shollar, staged a shortened version of *Swan Lake* for Diaghilev that became the basis for later one-act versions of the ballet. From 1921 to 1935 he also appeared with the Ida Rubinstein Company, Karsavina-Vilzak Company, Bronislava Nijinska's company, and as premier danseur, ballet master, and choreographer at the State Opera House in Riga, Latvia. In 1936 he joined René Blum's Ballet Russe de Monte Carlo and appeared as premier danseur at the Metropolitan Opera House in New York during the 1936–37 season, when George Balanchine was the choreographer. He began teaching at the School of American Ballet, established the Vilzak-Shollar School of Ballet in 1940, and later taught at the Ballet Russe de Monte Carlo School in New York City. He and his wife taught at the Washington School of Ballet in Washington, D.C., for two years before going to San Francisco to teach at the San Francisco Ballet School in 1965.

BARBARA FALLIS was born in Denver but grew up in London, where she received her elementary instruction and made her professional debut with the Vic-Wells (now Royal) Ballet. The war forced her family home to the States, and while still a teenager, she joined the corps de ballet of Ballet Theater, soon rising to the rank of soloist. She danced principal roles with The Ballet Alicia Alonso in Cuba (where she also married Richard Thomas) and returned to the United States to join the New York City Ballet in 1953. During her career Miss Fallis studied and performed with such great teachers and choreographers as Ninette de Valois, Nicholas Sergeyev, Anatole Vilzak, Ludmilla Shollar, Michel Fokine, Antony Tudor, Jerome Robbins, and George Balanchine. Among her most memorable roles were the Waltz in *Les Sylphides*, Calliope in *Apollo*, Princess Aurora in *Aurora's Wedding*, the Queen of the Wilis in *Giselle*, Lucile Grahn in *Pas de Quatre*, and Pigtails in *Graduation Ball*. Miss Fallis retired from the stage in 1958 to begin her teaching career. She helped found the Thomas-Fallis School with her husband and served as ballet mistress for Eliot Feld's American Ballet Company, which was based at their school. At her death in 1980 she was a codirector of The New York School of Ballet and U.S. Terpsichore (the school's resident company, founded in 1975).

Barbara Fallis

as the Queen of the Wilis in GISELLE

DATE

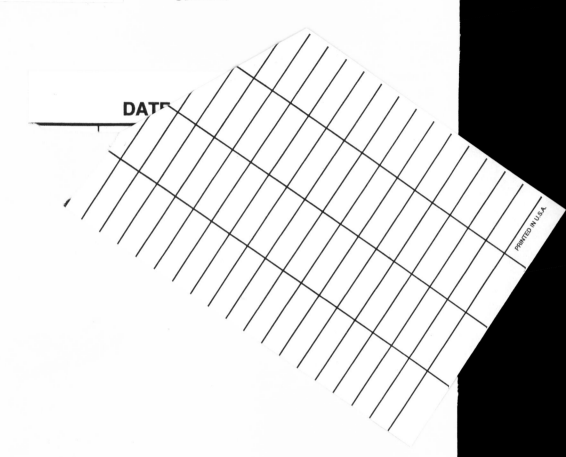

PRINTED IN U.S.A.